Edges

More Aster(ix) Anthologies

Dirty Laundry
Fall 2017

Kitchen Table Translation
Summer 2017

Best of Kweli
Spring 2017

What We Love
Fall 2016

Atravesando
Spring 2016

available for order wherever books are sold

Aster(ix) Journal

presents

Edges

Fall 2018

***

Edited by
Angie Cruz & Marta Lucía Vargas

BLUE SKETCH PRESS | PITTSBURGH

See page 101 for individual copyright information/acknowledgments.

Published via Blue Sketch Press, Pittsburgh.
www.bluesketchpress.com

Edges: An Aster(ix) Anthology / Aster(ix) Journal
Edited by Angie Cruz and Marta Lucía Vargas—1st ed.
ISBN (print) 978-1-942547-09-9 (trade paperback)
1-942547-09-9 (ISBN-10)
Cover art is detail from "Sky" by Laylah Ali, gouache on paper, 2014.
Cover Design by Little Owl Creative.
Copy-Edited by Joseph N. Welch III.

First Edition: September 2018

Printed in the United States of America
9 8 7 6 5 4 3 2 1

Aster(ix) Journal

www.asterixjournal.com

Aster(ix) is usually published 2-3 times a year in print with additional content online. **Aster(ix)** is funded in part by the Dietrich School of Arts and Sciences and the Department of English at University of Pittsburgh.

Contents

Edge

Nathalie Handal

> "A woman is perfected."
> Sylvia Plath

She is bare.
She is open.
Petals around her neck,
the moon on her shoulders,
she stares at the world,
takes it to the edge of
all the words
men weren't able to invent.

To Rachel

The Reservation

Nathalie Handal

If you don't understand
your homeland
hunger makes it all clear

Race Chronicle en Bref

Nathalie Handal

Every time you ask my color
the world is totally silent
and any crack in the song
is not half a dream
it's an entire country incomplete

Bad Muslim

Leila Nadir

I

I didn't want to pray. I didn't want to read the Qur'an. And I didn't want to fast. Performances required of me daily, annually. To not eat, to move my eyes over Arabic letters, to stand up, bend down, prostrate, get up, sit on my knees, thank God. I didn't believe it mattered. I didn't believe in Allah. And I didn't want to cover my hair for a supposedly benevolent, magnificent being, or read the words being delivered, via Angel Gabriel, to the illiterate Prophet Mohammed, the most unlikely of chosen ones. But I moved my body as required, wrapped my Qur'an in silk scarves, and put my breakfast down when the sun came up. Life was a charade, orchestrated to please authority. Prayer rugs were shifted, the Qur'an opened and closed, the wazu vase filled and emptied to look like water had poured from its spout. Water wiped across my forehead with my fingers, just enough to dampen my bangs, to make it look like I'd completed my ablutions. Signs. Symbols. A theatrical production staged to keep the peace.

Islam, for me, was a distorted, two-culture family drama, in which my parents played an unspoken game of high-stakes chess with one another, enacted in small moves, one square at a time, trying to gain territory, to win over, influence, control the kids, steer them toward or away from Allah. One was honest with his plans, hiding nothing. He said, This is what I want. The other was surreptitious, deploying spies, planning a coup, rearranging her pawns when he looked away.

Religion is complicated. And when a religion is under attack like Islam, when Muslims' lives are devalued and individual acts of violence indict millions, when women who cover their hair are threatened and persecuted because females everywhere must let everyone see their black yellow brown white hair, or else they are terrorists or not free, I wonder if this is the moment I should tell my story.

My childhood religious instruction went sort of like this:

On the Matter of Chadars (BTW This Is Not a Misspelling: *Chadar* Reflects the Afghan Persian [*Dari*] Pronunciation of چادر, the Pronunciation I Grew Up with, Said *chaw-Der*, which Almost Rhymes with my Last Name, *naw-Dir*, If Said Correctly, With a Fluttery, Rolling-R Emphasis on the Last Syllable, as Opposed to the Iranian Persian [*Farsi*] Pronunciation *Chador*)

Father: We're going to the mosque. Where's your chadar?
Mother: Headscarves are stupid.
Father: Fix your chadar. I can see your hair. How many times do I have to tell you?
Mother: Why do women wear headscarves? And why not men? How come men's hair doesn't have to be hidden?
Father: Women wear chadars to protect themselves.
Mother: Oh, so men can't control themselves around women's bodies, they are total maniacs, and women have to hide behind fabric so they don't get hurt? Look around America. I don't see a bunch of men attacking women because their hair is showing, do you?

I need to clarify: this back-and-forth dramatic reproduction does not refer to any real conversation held between my Afghan, Muslim father and my Slovak-American, latent Catholic mother. My parents did not deliver these statements in the spirit of debate or how-should-we-raise-the-kids discussion. Their pro- or anti- Islam stances were not even uttered in each other's presence, at least not exactly or directly. My father delivered his pronouncements to his children, in the "public" space of the home, which, for a patriarch, is wherever, whenever. No need for self-censorship. His law, his rule. Sometimes relayed gently, *Come here, let me explain.* Sometimes dropped down from above in the form of wall-shaking commands that made his children scramble and pretend they had something to do in another room. So, although he wasn't addressing my mother, she heard all.

My mother expressed her opinions privately, when my father wasn't around. After hours, so to speak. She was a teacher at the same school attended by my siblings and me, so our schedules were coordinated, our movements aligned. Plenty of Mom-kid time while my father was at work. When we returned home in the afternoon, at the end of our school day, my mother chipped away at my father's faith while warming dinner at the stove, letting me and my siblings catch up on all the TV shows he didn't allow. (When I was a teenager, she secretly recorded *Saturday Night Live* for me with the VCR—from our tiny New York State living room, NYC was already calling me.) In the dark early evenings of winter, when the sun would set at 4:30pm, she casually questioned the oddities of Afghan culture while handing us ornaments to hang on our plastic Christmas tree before he got home to object. (Once it was laden with crude ceramic ornaments made by his children stabbing away at clay in art class, how could he order the tree taken down?) While my father was pressing his foot to the gas pedal, changing lanes on Rochester's 490, cruising down 441, headed home to a split-level ranch in rural Wayne County, his family was living a life he couldn't imagine. His home in the country was full of Americans who loved Christmas and un-Islamic TV. It was full of Americans who shifted to our own special version of Afghan theater the moment he opened the front door.

Salaam Baba jaan! Yes, we said our prayers, yes, we read a page of the Qur'an, yes, yes. Let's eat dinner, *Bişmallah-i-rahman-i-rahim.*

And he smiled, so pleased. He was proud. He didn't know.

My father was consistent. Or maybe I should say he was transparent. Not because he tried to be but because he couldn't help it. His needs, loves, fears, paranoia, he flung them around the house—the way a toddler clenches his fists and screams because he doesn't have the skills to be more diplomatic. The world was good/bad, moral/immoral, black/white. Afghan/not. Emotions, hopelessly, painfully bare. (Do you love me?) And my mother was a puddle of distracted grey. I looked in her eyes, I tried all the time to initiate a meeting, a spontaneous one-on-one, *Hey, it's me*, but they always bounced unavailable. My mother lived one way in my father's presence, another when he wasn't around. Please the patriarch, roll your eyes behind his back. Lessons for her children on how to live a double life, never addressing what was really going on. It was like grade school: she and I had a nasty clique, spreading rumors, picking on the weak kid, playing nice when an adult—the principal, the lunch lady—walked by. My father was the weak one and he was the authority.

About Sunday School, which Most Local Muslims Believed Should Really Have Been Saturday School, Because Sunday School Sounded Too Christian, But the Mosque Leadership, in the 1980s, Decided, Despite Fervent Disgruntlement, Better to Align the Calendar of the Islamic Center Of Rochester ("I.C.R." for Short) with Regular American School Schedules, so Extra-Curricularly Inclined Muslim Kids Could Compete on Saturdays with their

American Classmates in Soccer Games, Wrestling Matches, Science Fairs, Chess Tournaments, and Spelling Bees (This Policy Has Since Changed)

Baba: Dr. Malik says the new mosque in Rochester is ready to open.

Mom: Religion. Everyone getting together to worship a god they can't see. Have you ever seen this Allah? Where's the evidence?

Baba: No more meeting in the basement at Dr. Malik's house. What a wonderful day. Rochester opens its first mosque!

Mom: Dr. Malik—he seems like an arrogant man. Where's his wife? What does she do? Have you ever seen her when you were at his house studying the Qur'an?

Baba: And the mosque has started Sunday School classes!

Mom: My parents made me go to Catholic School on weekends. The nuns liked to hit kids with rulers. Right here, on my knuckles, like this.

Baba: I signed you up for Mrs. Bakari's class for 11-13 year olds.

Mom: Who is Mrs. Bakari? All the mosque teachers are Pakistani housewives with no education, bored women looking for something to do. I wouldn't trust them to teach children.

Baba: I'm disappointed you got a 60% on your test on the life of Prophet Mohammed. This is a very serious topic. Prophet Mohammed, peace be upon him, led a life that is a model for all Muslims.

Mom: Don't worry about that quiz. You read a long book, poorly written, with spelling mistakes, and she quizzed you on three random facts hidden in two paragraphs. That's not how you make a test.

Baba: And Mrs. Bakari tells me you haven't been memorizing your surahs.

Mom: Memorization is not how kids learn, memorizing chapters word

> for word that they can't even understand. What do you even get out of that? Do you even know what any of it means? Maybe Mrs. Bakari should teach you Arabic before she requires you to memorize a bunch of Qur'an chapters.

The mosque's special school and Sunday prayers colonized half our weekend, which was a real tax on my schedule. By the time I was a teenager, I didn't care about being a good Muslim, praying, memorizing, chadar-ing, and all that. I was a Huge Nerd, and by high school, I was obsessed with "getting into a good college." I'd rather have been reading, and re-reading, a chapter of white-washed American history from a state-sanctioned textbook all weekend than praying at the mosque. I had a plan, and it took time: perfect grades → win a full-ride scholarship to a college faraway → escape my parents' house → achieve independence. But attending Shouldn't-Be-Sunday School was non-negotiable. I didn't even feel I could fake sick. Plus the future of Afghanistan depended on my family.

My father was sort of the leader of the local Afghan community at the time. He was the most assimilated, the most American, the one with the American wife and the four Honor Roll children, the one who'd actually chosen to go to college in the U.S., and to move here permanently, before the war with the Soviets had even broken out. But he was also extremely patriotic. When the Cold War, and the Russian tanks and the American rocket launchers, denied him the option to return home, he became obsessed with saving Afghanistan, its people, its culture. He sponsored refugees and helped them adapt to American life. He wrote our congresswoman about expediting immigration applications for not only family members but also total strangers. He wrote his senators. He called newspapers and news stations and gave interviews. He provided his perspective on "Escaping the War in Afghanistan," which was the title of an article in Rochester's *Democrat &*

Chronicle, and I've even found a quotation from him in the *Los Angeles Times*, about the Soviet withdrawal of troops in 1989. Locally, he took it upon himself to ensure that all area Afghan kids didn't "lose their culture."

Every Sunday morning, my father drove into Rochester with his four children and gathered up all the Afghan youth he could find to deliver to the mosque's Shouldn't-Be-Sunday School. We picked up confused Afghan refugee kids who spoke no English and lived in furniture-less apartments with their parents in crime-ridden inner-city neighborhoods. We picked up the snazzily dressed offspring of Western-educated Afghan bourgeoisie who resided in sterile housing-development cul-de-sacs. When some Egyptians at the mosque realized my father was driving around town, acting as a self-appointed Mosque Busdriver, willingly picking up any young Muslims he could fit into his van, we started picking up their kids too. Our services targeted spiritually imperiled Afghan boys and girls, but ultimately, we made no distinctions regarding class, color, ethnicity, nationality, or dialect. No matter if there weren't enough seats to go around, no matter if we had long ago run out of seatbelts. Equal opportunity pile-up. If you were Muslim, climb aboard my father's Volkswagen van. I called it the Afghan Cara-van.

On our way out of the house into the caravan on Sunday mornings, my siblings and I marched down the stairs with our backpacks filled with Qur'ans for memorizing surahs and typed-up, photocopied reading assignments[1]. I already had wrapped my chadar around my

---

1 I avoided memorizing surahs, but I loved reading those little booklets. They came in the form of photocopies of photocopies, authors unknown, publishers long gone, stapled and bound at copy shops and sold for $5 a bundle in the mosque's library-store. These were our only English access to Islamic history, to the details of the life of Prophet Mohammed, to the cities of Mecca and Medina

brown, Slovak-Afghan hair, and I watched my little brother leap down the steps, his head of curls bouncing like an advertisement for body-building miracle shampoo. I fantasized about shaving my head. Would that be modest enough for my father? If my hair was so controversial, why not lose it altogether? Why did I have to keep my hair long and then wear a scarf over it? Wasn't that a circuitous route to modesty? And why, on Sundays, did my father make me put it on before I was even out the door, as if the mosque grounds, and Allah's gaze, suddenly extended into our front yard on Sundays, which, of course, was the Christian holy day?

I blamed the chadar for making my scalp itch. I was always sticking a finger under the fabric to do a bit of casual scratching. But the irritation was probably more due to my poor hygiene, because Afghan chadars are loose and flowing, not restrictive at all. As a teenager, I washed my hair everyday. Blow-dry, mousse, curl, hairspray, all the processes and chemical products required of American females in the eighties in order to prove we'd successfully conquered nature and gravity. But on Sundays, who cared? I just wrapped my hair with one of the chadars sent by my aunts from Afghanistan, an oily, flattened, matted mess, full of hairspray flakes. The sign of women's anti-feminism smothering my scalp, I thought, the counter-sign to my mother's puffy blond highlighted Clairol liberation.

My mother didn't join us at the mosque on Sundays. She abstained with the moral righteousness of a nineteenth-century teetotaler, her childhood Catholicism infusing her adult faith in the secular. She didn't drink. She wouldn't touch alcohol. She believed mothers were pure,

---

circa 600 A.D. Full of folklore and legends and narrative designed for kids, these stapled booklets never got around to declaring moral rules, except for No Killing Spiders, because a spider once saved Prophet Mohammed's life, and I've never killed one (purposefully) since.

all-knowing saints (like the Virgin Mary, whom, ironically, she didn't believe in anymore). And she was too smart to believe in God or spend time in the mosque. Virtue through abstinence, the Catholic way.

But she truly couldn't wait for her children to leave for the Shouldn't-Be-Sunday School. She thought a mosque education was a bunch of indoctrination, brainwashing her son and three daughters to believe hocus-pocus and not think straight, but she paused her criticism on Sundays so she could have the house to herself. A Special Ed teacher Monday through Friday, she managed a multi-grade classroom of elementary-age students with learning disabilities, behavioral outbursts, and not enough to eat. Sundays were her only break from teaching kids and mothering kids and kids kids kids. While my father was beeping the horn from the driveway, summoning his Muslim student-children to the Afghan Cara-van, my mother was already deep into the couch with a cup of coffee. Thank God her husband was taking the kids to the mosque. Not yet changed out of her robe, she had *The New York Times* open on her lap, scanning headlines for the pleasure she was about to have soaking up culture and news, and the science section, with the proof and experiments and latest knowledge based on reports and fact.

My little sisters announced our leaving: "Bye, Mom!"

I was afraid she would see me in my chadar, which she told me was stupid, and bad for women, and here I was covering my hair in our living room. What would she think?

Eyes on the paper, mug to her lips, she didn't look up. "Bye, kids!"

Regarding my Name, which Was Almost Zainab, but Was Legally Christine, and Temporarily Leila, Then Ultimately Aliyeh (and in My Early Twenties, During a Series of Art Performances, Kristina Mohammed, a Pseudonym Invented for What Should Now Be Obvious Reasons) until I Petitioned an Oneida County Judge, in New York State, Placed a Notice in a Newspaper, and Settled the

Matter at Age 35, When I Combined Part of the Name my Mother Had Signed on my Birth Certificate, Christine Michelle Nadir, with the Name My Father Chose for Me, the Name of a Mythological Female Hero, so that I Became Leila Christine Nadir

Mom: Your father was in Afghanistan when you were born, and he sent a letter asking me to name you Zainab, after his mother, but I couldn't see you as Zainab. How many nice girl names start with the letter Z?

Baba: Christine—I'm not sure if that's a good name for a Muslim girl. I'm going to call you Leila. Leila jaan.[2]

Mom: Your father's letter arrived too late anyway. I'd already filled out the birth certificate.

Baba: Listen while I will tell you the story of Leila and Majnun.

Mom: I picked out the name *Christine* way back when I was a teenager. I remember writing it down in one of my notebooks, doodling it when I was bored in class. I knew one day I'd have a daughter, and I'd name her *Christine Michelle*. It was my favorite name. For my first-born daughter.

Baba: Leila and Majnun are the Romeo and Juliet of Persian Literature.

Mom: How do you feel about your father changing your name

---

2 Note to non-Persian readers: *Jaan* is not pronounced like the female name Jan. Persian has frequent "aw" vowel sounds. Imagine jaan as a quickly said "lawn" but with a j: jawn. Explaining the linguistic and cultural significance of *jaan* is nearly impossible and maybe some other time I will try, but for now, just know, it's added to names as a term of endearment. It can feel sincere, sentimental, and meaningful, though it can also feel mandatory at the same time. To drop it off a name can be significant, offensive, sending a message. It's as if using *jaan* automatically makes you a sweeter person, polite, with manners. But don't take my word for any of this. I'm a Half-ghan.

suddenly? You're ten years old, and you've always been Christine.

Baba: Leila's and Majnun's families wouldn't let them be together, and when Majnun couldn't be with Leila, he went crazy and died.

Mom: Tell your father he can't just change your name. Your name has always been Christine. For ten years. He can't just change it without asking you.

Baba: *Majnun* means *diwaneh*, crazy, mad. Without Leila, Majnun went insane.

Mom: Did you talk to your father?

Baba: Ahmed Zahir wrote a song about a girl named Leila. Let me see if I can find a recording in my tapes. *Leili Leili Leili jaan, jaan...*

Mom: What did your father say?

I was Shakespeare's Juliet of Persia, someone to fall in love with, and even though, already in elementary school, I was barely allowed to talk to boys, if I did talk to them they would probably go crazy because I was so lovely and magical and fine. I had an Afghan pop song all about me. It made me want to stare at my reflection in the mirror: Is it, could it be, true?

But an injustice had been committed. I complained to my father, as instructed, and he agreed to stop calling me Leila but only if I picked out a new name more appropriate for a Muslim girl. On a sheet of ruled paper torn from one of my notebooks, he made a list, thirty or so suggestions, the original Persian and the English spelling side-by-side, and I pretended to study and compare. When he wasn't around, I dutifully held up the list to my mother.

Which name?

She pointed at *Aliyeh*. "At least this one makes sense."

My mother could read and write basic Persian, from lessons my father had given her long ago. Before their marriage became an epic battle for their children's souls, they must have collaborated a bit. She could see that *Aliyeh* started with the letter ع (pronounced "ein," a guttural A-type sound, from the back of the throat), like the rest of my siblings' names. My father was out of the country when I was born, but he had been in the States for all of theirs, at Newark-Wayne Community Hospital, in a rural delivery room, where, when my parents discovered the sex of their newborns, he'd suggest Persian names and my mother picked out her favorite, always settling on names that began with all variations of the name of Prophet Mohammed's cousin and son-in-law, the first Shia Imam, Ali.

Christine remained my name among Americans, at my American public school, within my mother's Slovak-American, Catholic family. Aliyeh became my name at the mosque, the name my Afghan family would call me for perpetuity, the name my Afghan father thought I picked out but really it was the orchestration all along of his American wife, angry that, when he hadn't been in the country for my delivery, he deigned to reject her Christine. But the matter of my name wasn't over. The tension about my name made my brother and sisters so uncomfortable that they avoided calling me anything at all. Christine offended my father, and also, it seemed, Islam and Allah. "*Aliyeh b'go*!" he'd yell across the house whenever he heard a whisper of *Christine*, the same way he'd yell, "*Farsi b'go*! Speak Persian! No English!" And *Aliyeh*, though my mother chose it, was treated by her as a betrayal, another disappointment in a lifetime of this-is-not-how-my-life-was-supposed-to-turn-out.

My youngest sister found a solution, a sneak maneuver proving that, even at three years old, she had learned how to navigate my parents' cold war.[3] She and I were close. Though I was only eight years

3 This may be a good time to mention that I have published an essay, titled "Cold War," about how my parents met, in *North American Review* 298.3 (Summer 2013).

older than her, I imagined she was my daughter. When I pushed her down the street in her cheap, wobbly-wheel stroller, I believed I looked so mature and capable at four feet tall, so big and grown-up, that I was sure, any moment, a stranger would look lovingly at my baby and remark upon my wonderful maternal nature, "Oh, what a nice mom you are." My baby sister and I slept in the same bed, and every night I rubbed her back until she fell asleep, an arrangement my mother encouraged because this sister was a bed-wetter and this meant that almost every night I awoke to urine in the sheets, and because I was such a good mom, I'd strip the mattress, rinse her off in the bathtub, and clean up the mess on my own without waking our parents. Having no name to address me cut through our intimacy. It's like opening your mouth to call out to a loved one in a dream, but you've forgotten their name. So she called me Sister. Nobody could object.[4]

On the Topic of Inter-Marriage, that is, Whether Muslims Can Marry Non-Muslims, or Put Another Way, Whether "Believers" Can Marry "Non-Believers" (A Somewhat Related Side-story: At Shouldn't-Be-Sunday School, I Learned that during Prophet Mohammed's Time the "Non-Believers" Were Actually "Paganists," and They Liked to Mold Gold into the Shapes of Animals and Worship these Objects like Powerful Gods, and though I Didn't Learn this Next Part in our Sunni-Dominated Mosque, my Father Told Me that This Is Why Shi'a Muslims, which Is What We Were, Prayed with Our Hands Down at our Sides, rather than Clasped

4 Lest my readers fall into any sentimental delusions about the power of sibling bonding in the face of parental instability, let me un-delude you: this sister hasn't spoken to me in ten years. "Unhappy families are conspiracies of silence. The one who breaks the silence is never forgiven." Jeanette Winterson wrote that.

Together at our Hearts Like Sunnis at the Mosque, Because Fake-Muslim Paganists Used to Place Idols in their Sleeves When They Prayed, and When I Heard This, I Thought, Wasn't I Still Fake-Praying Too, even with My Hands Down, Worshipping Something Else?)

Baba: The Qur'an says that Muslim men can marry non-believing women, but if the situation is reversed, if a Muslim woman wants to marry a non-Muslim man, Allah says, that is not allowed.[5]

Mom: What if you are an Afghan in America going to college as a graduate student, and you never even mention Islam to your American girlfriend, you drink beer at parties, you marry her in a Catholic ceremony, in a church with a priest and all that, and you have children together, and then years later, you decide, all of a sudden, that you are actually quite religious and your children have to be good Muslims and go to the mosque? What does Allah say about that?

Baba: Allah allows men to marry women who are not Muslims because it is a strategy for gaining followers of Islam.

Mom: I guess your brother can marry whomever he likes then. Too bad for you and your sisters. You'll need to find Muslim men. Maybe you can join a Muslim Student Association or something? Maybe there are some boys at the mosque you like?

Baba: Allah understands men and women and how they are different.

---

5 My father was actually wrong about this. The Qur'an states that a Muslim woman can marry any man of the book. I have never read the Qur'an in English, only in Arabic, which I didn't understand, so I have to thank my dear friend Zohra Saed, who has a beautiful name starting with the letter Z, for sharing this fact with me. "So any one of the four holy books," she wrote me in an email after reading a draft of this essay. "It's patriarchal culture that hides that."

We have to trust his judgment. Women are more likely to convert to their husbands' religion. Not the other way around.

Mom: Is that what your father said? I guess it's just a matter of time before I convert. He's really persuading me. And watch out, because, you know, American converts are the worst, the strictest, the most religious ones, like Kaka Nima's wife.

Kaka Nima's wife, whose actual name I never knew, scared me.[6] Her

---

6 The following note about Kaka Nima's wife's name is not only for non-Persians although it initially reads that way: "Kaka" means uncle in Persian, a language spoken by both Iranians (Farsi dialect) and by Afghans (Dari dialect), and children preface adult's names with *kaka* or *khaleh* (aunt) out of respect, creating a more familial feeling than distant titles like "Mr." and "Mrs." In addition, proper names are often replaced by job titles—Afghans called my father *Engineer*—or family references, especially, it seemed, for women, such as "Hamid's mother" or "Hamayun's wife." (Hence, Kaka Nima and Kaka Nima's wife.) In my family, the Afghan members called my mother *zen-maamaa*, which means "Uncle's Wife." (*Maamaa* also means uncle. *Zen* means wife.) My father's sister, my aunt Ammeh jaan, whom I will discuss later in this essay, called my mother *zen-maamaa*, and her children, aged toddler through teenager, did the same, all out of respect. This practice, however, annoyed my mother. Why couldn't she be called by her God-given name? She was also disturbed that the Persian word for "wife" was the same word used for "woman": *zen*. So essentially, to my mother's grumpy ear, these little kids were calling her "uncle's woman." This was all a bit too un-feminist for her taste, and probably just too sexist and too Afghan, and another way to point out the superiority of her progressive American ways. Perhaps she complained, because at some point, *zen-maamaa* was replaced by a new name my father made up for her, and he instructed his nieces and nephews to replace *zen-maamaa* with *gul-jaan*, essentially *Dear Flower*. My mother, the sweet flower. Was this my father's joke? Or another

husband, obviously named Kaka Nima, was my father's best buddy at the mosque. They were the only regular Persians in attendance (though Kaka Nima was from Iran). They sat cross-legged on the floor, side-by-side, in the men's area of the prayer hall. The beads of their *tasbeh* rolled through their fingers while they waited for the *azaan* to call them to prayer. The two men had much in common even beyond language and culture. They both had thinning hair with unabashed combovers and middle-aged bellies, not big but definitely, roundly there. They wore identical fashion, switching between traditional attire (*perhan tumban*) some days and the mid-managerial professional look (pressed slacks and tucked-in, button-down shirts) on others. And they both had pale, blond American wives, whom they'd met during their liberal college years, and a string of light brown half-Persian children as a result. They differed, however, in that Kaka Nima's wife had converted. She'd followed her husband's lead, as Allah predicted, as Baba said would happen. And my mother was a hold-out.

To me, Kaka Nima's wife seemed like my mother's evil twin, like she could have been my mom with just one turn or twist of fate, *khoda nekoneh*, God Forbid, the American woman who became an official Muslim with an official hijab who took Islam too seriously. More than anything, I feared her beady green eyes landing on me. Those eyes could sense religious infractions from afar, hone in from across a room, as if she were a stand-in for omniscient Allah. She pointed at wisps of hair peeking out from the loose headscarves of girls giggling in corners. (None of the Middle Eastern Moms did that.) Little boys chased each other maniacally in circles around our little upstate mosque, treating its perimeter like a racetrack, and she stood police-like, dead-center in their path, slowing their sprinting with her statuesque moral presence and disapproving glare. And when the mosque moms sold $1 pizza

---

instance of Afghan keeping-up-appearances?

over the kitchen counter to Shouldn't-Be-Sunday School students after *dhuhr* prayers, taking the dollar and looking the other way, Kaka Nima's wife busted the kids trying to slide an extra slice onto their plates. She is the one who discovered that the mosque guardian, a chubby man who lived in a tiny downstairs apartment, had hidden bacon in the mosque fridge. She mobilized the mosque moms into a raucous stampede, knocked on his door, and had him fired on the spot.

My mother came face-to-face with Kaka Nima's wife about four times every year, on Friday nights during the month of Ramadan, when Muslim families came together to pray and break their fasts with a communal dinner at the mosque. I'm not sure why my mother joined us for Iftar, but perhaps it was because my parents prided themselves on their traditional values. They prioritized eating every meal together as a family, albeit unhappily. (We must have unhappy dinners together!) For Iftar, my mother draped a chadar over her puffy, hair-sprayed hair, like a tent floating on a scaffolding of stiff curls, suspended an inch above her scalp. This nodding rejection at Muslim female humility got her through the mosque's double doors. Her lack of respect embarrassed me in front of my teachers, my classmates, but my father seemed grateful for the act, and he met her halfway. During Iftar, the men congregated on one side of the community room—I saw a mix of men's dull clothing at the far end, shades of brown, white, black fabric—and the women gathered on the other, with their pink orange purple green *shalwar kameez* and chadars. Everyone gender-segregated, except for some African-American families, my father and Kaka Nima, their American wives, and their children. We carried our paper plates and plastic forks to the tables set up on the balcony overlooking the prayer hall, a quiet mixed-gendered space away from the segregated, monochrome/multi-colored masses from Central Asia and the Middle East.

While eavesdropping on the adults' conversations, I taste-tested tiny forkfuls of the potluck dishes spooned onto my plate, having learnt by the time I was in my teens to identify the Pakistani dishes before their searing spices lit a flame in my mouth. Kaka Nima and my father filled their empty, fasting bellies, chatting while they chewed. What was the latest on Ronald Reagan, Khomeini, the mujahideen, when would Sunday School become Saturday School, how many goals did their daughters score in last week's soccer games, how was family in Afghanistan, in Iran, in Kabul, in Tehran, and in all the faraway places that exiles of their two homelands' revolutions had ended up. And my mother and Kaka Nima's wife sat across the table from each other, straining. Two American women with so much in common and so little to say. Porcelain-white skin, green eyes, Persian husbands, and chadars (sincere or not) over their blond hair. Women who had once talked to boys on the telephone, tried out for cheerleading teams, dressed in formal gowns for formal dances, all of which their Muslim daughters (fake or not) were now forbidden to do. I wonder if Kaka Nima's wife had also been Catholic, like my mother. The falling-so-easily into moral clarity, universal truth. Science and religion, the lab and the holy book. Back at the mosque on Sundays, without my mother beside me, I turned my face into my chadar and walked the other way whenever I saw Kaka Nima's wife. I was afraid she knew about my other life, that I was a fake Muslim, that I wore mini-skirts to regular school and my mother bought them for me and told me, don't worry, put them on after your father leaves for work. That I thought my chadar was stupid and on Sundays I didn't wash my hair and I had a dirty scalp. That I faked my period so I wouldn't have to pray, and I pretended to fast during Ramadan but sometimes ate small bites of whatever I wanted all day. If I wasn't careful, Kaka Nima's wife would focus her convert eyes on me, green laser-beams penetrating my soul, and she would say, "Your father might not know it, but I know. I know about the secret club you have with your mother, and I know what she says about me, and I know what she says about him."

II

My mother melted sugar in a sauce pan for *baklava.* She baked a crunchy layer of egg at the bottom of the *chalau.* She rolled little circles of dough out on the counter to make wheat pockets for fried *boulani,* filled with mashed potato and *nana,* a special variety of leeks grown by my father in our vegetable garden from seeds brought from Afghanistan. To make *mantu,* she bought a double boiler. "Now this is fancy," she said, pulling the stainless-steel parts from the manufacturer's box, the first gourmet appliance purchase, I bet, in the history of her Slovak immigrant family. I grew up immersed in Afghan cuisine prepared oddly enough, yet expertly, by my American mother, and while she baked *naan* one day, I remember, as a young girl, telling her a story I'd heard at the mosque about Allah and Paradise and the Day of Judgment. About how the graves in the cemetery would open, the dead would rise, start walking, and the sun would come closer and closer to the earth, until it was just above everyone's heads, and it would be so hot that humans would melt unless they were believers and then Allah would give them a special umbrella to protect them from the heat. I was worried my mother would be left behind, even worse, melted down, in pain, suffering. The stories taught by my earliest mosque teachers were simple stories, uncomplicated and accessible for young minds, with clear opposites—*believers unbelievers, Believers Unbelievers, BELIEVERS UNBELIEVERS*—categories best not told to children being raised in a bicultural home with two discordant parents.

I was still quite small—small enough that I could look down straight into the oven while standing upright—and I watched my mother bend to pull a sheet of golden naan off its baking rack, set it down on the stove top, and rub the end of a half-unwrapped stick of butter across the top. Up, down. The butter melted across the bread, glistening, the way it does on a hot cob of corn, and she asked me, Who told me this story? How did I know it was true? Could it be that Allah had communicated with me directly?

What couldn't be demonstrated by science, she said, proven with an experiment, based on fact, seen with her own eyes, she didn't believe. I opened my mouth to respond, but my faith had just crashed into her logic, my religion into her liberal secularism, my dutiful absorption of adult words into a new who-do-I-trust. I watched her push the buttered naan back in the oven and shut the door. She had twenty-four years on me, she was a teacher of elementary-age children. Did she feel my struggle to drag the pieces of a sentence into a presentable pile? I remember only shared silence, a wordless coexisting, as the steam of freshly baked bread filled in the air. My mother waited a few minutes for the butter to turn the naan's crust into a luxurious, toasty-creamy-crunchy crust. Then she bent down and swiftly pulled it out of the oven with a pot-holdered hand, all done, just the way her Muslim husband liked it.

III

The oven scene was my first memory of my childhood home quaking under the burden of religion. Islam was what could be grasped. It was made up of categories and labels that fit the frame. Islam was what could be grasped. It could be reduced to categories and labels that fit the frame, that covered over uncomfortable, inarticulable truths, the way politicians, in their stump speeches, scapegoat Islam today. Words about religion can be alibis, in private homes, in politics, in public policy, the excuses for the questions we don't want to ask because we're not going to like the answers.

An ongoing concern of my father's was that my mother—he wasn't sure how—was turning his children against him. My father had lost both his parents by the time he was eight years old. A boy without a mother, without a father, now a father with four kids, he was easily confused. I imagine he held rules in his fists, tightly, as tokens of cultural security. This is who he was, this is who his children would be, and if he opened his grip and passed down his Afghan bullet-points—Shouldn't-Be-Sunday School, prayers five times a day, fasting and Ramadan, Persian lessons (but only sometimes), chadars (but pretty much only at the mosque), no daughters talking to boys on the telephone (unless I absolutely had to discuss homework assignments because my teacher said: that story always worked for me), and no after-school activities, except for soccer, which he loved—then his son and daughters would be good people, they would love him, they would be like him, he wouldn't be alone. We wouldn't lose our culture. He wouldn't lose his culture.

But he was outplayed by an American teacher, who knew how to manage children and make life lessons fun and mix authority with being your best friend, who knew how to combine ice cream and spaghetti and a Golden Oldies Dance Party with a dose of secularism. Home court advantage.

IV

One of my last memories of my parents' religious problems took place years later, when I was a teenager, on a Shouldn't-Be-Sunday School day. The weather was pleasant because, though I was wearing my chadar and Afghan *perhan tumban* for a day of humbleness at the Islamic Center, I remember my mother was wearing a pair of cut-off jean shorts and a white t-shirt. I never really enjoyed weekly classes at the mosque. Kaka Nima's wife's beady green eyes were always around the corner, my scalp itched, and I had to memory-cram surahs before tests to avoid becoming The Bad Girl with the American Mother. But I had a friend, Fareshta, from Pakistan, a fellow nerdy girl whom I met while being nerdy together during our teenage-level class. I always looked forward to spending the day with her.

The Caravan for Afghan Youth at Risk of Losing their Culture was preparing to take off on its series of cross-county suburban-urban pickups in honor of Allah. I was in the front seat, chadar in place. Seat belts buckled. Notebooks, Qur'ans, pens, pencils properly stowed in backpacks, the van's engine cranked—when, after a night of screaming and fighting and wall-punching and keep-the-kids-up-all-night (my Walkman got me through those; I just kept on studying for that scholarship), my mother stomped down the sidewalk, barefoot, and stood in front of the van so it couldn't move without running her over, and stared at her husband through the windshield, yelling, "I'm not letting you go!" My parents were finally talking directly to each other about religion.

This conversation happened.

Baba: Please move. We have to go.

Mom: No, I'm tired of the mosque mosque mosque mosque mosque mosque mosque.

Baba: Stop this. We are leaving. You know you take my children away from me everyday but I am only taking my children to the mosque.

Mom: What are you talking about?

Baba: They love you more than me.

Mom: Children don't do that. I never once asked myself which parent I loved more, my mother or my father. That's crazy.

Baba: You don't support me. You don't understand me.

Mom: If you feel them pulling away, it's because of your rules. This is America. You're driving them away by forcing Islam on them.

Baba: I want them to be good people, good Muslims. Afghans are Muslims.

Mom: Then why are you the only one driving all the Muslim kids in the entire city of Rochester to the mosque? None of your friends care. They don't make their kids read the Qur'an every morning, or pray five times a day. It's too much!

Baba: They love you more than me. I can feel it.

Mom: Children need to learn different cultures, not just yours. They need to be exposed to different ways of life, and then they can decide for themselves. That's the best way.

Baba: Islam is the Afghan way. I want them to know my culture.

Mom: Well, what about my culture?

Baba: This whole country is your culture.

Mom: Then why don't the children learn my religion? I went to church every Sunday!

Baba: Be honest. You have no religion.

Mom: I'm not going to let you take my children to the mosque anymore! It's all Islam. Why don't I take them to church?

Baba: I never said they couldn't go to church.

Mom: Well, I'm taking them today. It's Sunday. Kids, let's go, we're going to church.

My mother looked at me, in the front seat, through the windshield of the van. Her ally. Her secret team-member. But I didn't move. My father did nothing. My three siblings froze. Church? Really? Whaaa? Wasn't religion the antithesis of truth? She had switched the rules of the game when her strategy didn't work.

She sank to the ground, her head between her knees, crying. It was one of those moments when an avalanche of repressed emotions buries you deep, because you didn't take care when you should've, and you don't know how it all started, and now you are alone, gasping for air, with nothing to hold onto. It had never been about God or science, about church or freedom, or teaching her children about multiculturalism and pluralistic perspectives. It was about her marriage, and her endless problems with my father, their deadlocked relationship, their Catholic-Muslim refusal to divorce. The way he scared us at times, with rules and commands and his superior physical strength. His recent edict that the only college I could attend was the nearby University of Rochester, so I could live at home under his supervision. If I didn't get that scholarship, the army was my backup way out. But none of that was discussed. And neither was the fact that he didn't listen to her needs. Or his children's needs. And how she needed his approval. She was unable to stop pleasing him despite her growing rage. Always a good girl. And the children were the way to punish him for what he hadn't done right. If he wasn't the husband he was supposed to be, and if she couldn't break out, she would make her children express her emotions, her judgments, and he wouldn't know it, and it would be a secret, but the children would be hers. She would be the favorite parent, the always-right mom. She would show him she had been on higher moral ground all along, affirmed by their children's votes.

My mother once told me I would love going to college. I was opening university brochures at my desk, hoping I could go somewhere beyond Rochester, somewhere far from my parents' home, and she used an adjective I never forgot. "It's so neat," she said, "to meet people from other places." Neat? It was if my mother's mental-world was so full-of-sameness, so believing in white, that she forgot that the neat guy she met in college was my father, and I was growing up with him, that I was his half-Afghan daughter, bilingual in English and Persian, that I spent weekends at the mosque in Rochester, hanging out with Pakistani, Egyptian, African-American, and Iranian Muslim kids. I might pass for white, and she might have called me Christine, but I wasn't in her club. For my mom, I was one of the neat ones.

My father was a stranger in his own house, and my mother was sobbing in front of a caravan of neat people. One neat husband and four neat kids.

V

While I was being raised Muslim by one parent, I was taught by the other to believe that Muslims were one way, that they blindly followed a book and didn't think for themselves, that religion could be trumped by non-religion, by reason and science, so I couldn't be Muslim, there was no way. My childhood was a Muslim-enough act to keep my father content and an anti-Muslim promise to my mother that I was like her, and not like her disappointing husband.

All the while, the Muslims in my life welcomed me into their homes, into their kitchens, their backyards, teaching me, slowly, even before I recognized the lessons, what religion and culture really mean when they are not judged as monolithic ways of life or the outdated precursors of supposedly rational modes of thought, when they are not pitted against secular blind faith.

The rituals, the spiritual patterns, the sacred days. The lived, evolving, collective memory, transplanted to America but increasingly, slowly, at home. Anchors of identity as light as the breath of the everyday. You only feel them when you are displaced.

One Ramadan, I was helping my aunt, Ammeh jaan, with preparations for the evening meal that would break our family's collective fasting, I saw her somewhat unapologetically (her back was barely turned) stuff a handful of rice into her mouth and gulp it down with a sip of water. The muscles in my face went slack. My God-fearing Muslim aunt. During Ramadan, she was not supposed to eat. And no drinking, not even water, sunup to sundown. When she turned around and saw my look, she put her finger to her lips, smiled, and winked, "Don't tell." This was my father's devout sister, married in Kabul before she'd even finished high school, always in traditional *perhan tumban*. She never left her house without a chadar over her hair. ("Have you noticed?" my mother would always ask, nudging me, making sure I saw.) And now this aunt was smiling at the naiveté of her teenage American niece. She told her daughter Robina to give me a bowl of rice. I probably looked pale, my blood sugar low, because I sort of, kind of, fasted. I never gave up certain gestural links that connected my two selves. Life would have been too dissociative otherwise. I ate a little when I fasted, thought about Allah a little when I prayed, read a few sentences before I turned another page of the Qur'an, balancing my father and my mother, good Muslim, bad Muslim, a Catholic-style Limbo, not stricken, not saved.

When I pretended to have my period in order to skip prayers at the mosque, it was the idea of my cousin Madina, another of my Ammeh jaan's children. Madina pulled me by the hand to the mosque balcony, and below us everyone prostrated, stood, sat, repeat, while we hung out in a couple of fold-out chairs, menstruating supposedly. Madina had been born in Afghanistan, then raised in Pakistan after her parents escaped the war, and now, at fifteen, a new arrival to the U.S., she was eager to figure this place out. She asked me about boys—I was her native informant, the explainer of local mores—how to act, what to say, what does this or that mean, should she call him back. Look, she said, pulling up her *tumban* to show me her legs, newly shaven, bare of hair, sexy brown smooth. All this I got behind, giving pointers as needed, but eventually Madina's fearless disobeying of her parents left me in the dust. My cousin couldn't be controlled. Even after she got caught sneaking out her window at night to meet up with an Italian boy (but not until she'd already done it a dozen times), and even after she moved into our house awhile to let her enraged father cool off, she liked to hum, behind her chadar, the popular hit "Bad Boy" by Miami Sound Machine. *Bad bad bad bad boy you make me feel so good.* Our parents had no clue about the words behind the melody.

My cousin Madina was the boy-craziest girl I ever knew, Muslim or otherwise, the one who took the most chances relative to the liberties allowed. And I have no doubt, on Judgment Day, that Allah will give her an air-conditioned umbrella to share with that Italian guy whom she happily married in a two-tone ceremony, with a quiet Muslim exchanging-of-vows in the mosque's prayer hall, officiated by an imam, and a lavish, dripping-with-lace, Afghan-Italian reception at a hotel with crystal chandeliers and dancing till midnight. And I'm sure her fake-fasting mother, Ammeh jaan, now grandmother to two Afghan-Italian-American kids, will be there, on her way to Paradise. And I'll be there too. Even though today I tell myself that practicing yoga and meditation are fine stand-ins for my childhood prayers, and weekend juice fasts are satisfactory updates to the sacrifices of Ramadan, and sending checks to the local farm sanctuary is a version of *zakaat*. Because I've always been a better Muslim, and more Afghan, than I thought.

You and the Pendulum

Rosa Alcalá

She held a chain with a crystal suspended from it over different parts of your body and asked questions. Sometimes you told her what you needed to know, more often she dangled the pendulum over an organ to interrogate, implicitly, its proper functioning. Even as her hand remained steady, the crystal would begin to swing from the chain in circles, clockwise or counterclockwise, giving a yes or no answer. These readings took place in her apartment, and although it was small and cluttered and had probably once been a cold-water flat, you wondered if it was rent controlled, because how else could she live there, in that inflated market. You were having problems with digestion, as you have since you were a kid, and she showed you how to massage your intestine, advising you: stay away from most nightshades. She sought a second opinion by holding the pendulum over one of the tomatoes on her kitchen table, and this seemed more efficient and less scary than a million needles pushed into the skin. But the question you waited to ask until the end was about the scientist with the British accent. Your gut told you it would only last through the summer, but as she held the pendulum and asked if he was your future, the chain and crystal began to vibrate and turn in small, then increasingly wider, circles, faster and faster in the direction of yes. You wrote her a check and headed for a payphone to tell your scientist about the diagnosis.

You to the Future

Rosa Alcalá

What would you have said to the future? Future, you will have no scientist in it. Future, your scientist was kissing a Canadian. Future, you could have told me, don't go to his apartment, depress the doorbell for many seconds, wait in his favorite diner around the corner, call him from the dark and humid underground of your last rumbling hope. But, Future, let me tell you something truly remarkable: there were payphones on subway platforms, which was great when you needed one, but if you needed one, things were often not so great. You were late for an interview or you wanted to be told, don't get on that train, I love you, come back to bed. No one on a subway payphone wanted to be told, "Hold on." You were lost, trying to buy weed, calling some guy's beeper. The receiver and keypad were archives of body-cum-city, and in these moments of disorientation, of numbers black and waxy and sticky, the pointer finger brought you closer to your desire with its impeccable memory. Future, I guess you already know that lovers feel their feelings wherever and whatever the mode. On the body, no longer at home. A screen the size of a palm. But in you, Future, no one will know what it's like to make a collect call, to reverse the charges. Or remember the Spanish poet who wrote an ode to his light bulb late one night in the kitchen.

from *The Proscenium*

Vi Khi Nao

3. Preface:

"At first, she[1] tries to carry the purse. She tries to insert the entire alphabet[2] into her purse.[3] At first, she tries to insert[4]..."
– Ambrosio LeAbsence

1

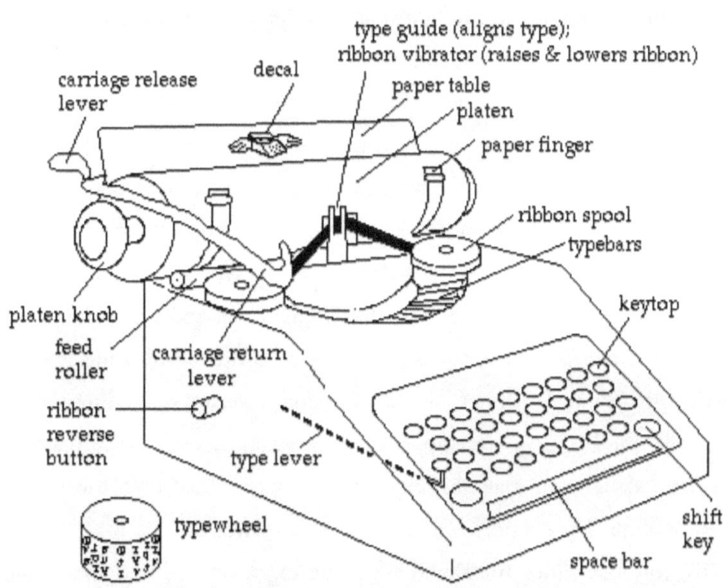

---

2 Valance is in her bedroom. After taking the typewriter to her bed, Valance takes apart the typewriter. She unlatches the carriage release lever, decal, platen knob, feed roller, ribbon reverse button, carriage return lever, type lever, space bar, shift keys, keytops, ribbon spools, paper finger, platen, paper table, ribbon vibrator, type guide, little bolts, and parts, and inserts them into a Christofle bread bag. She keeps the typebars, not in the bag, closer to her body. Valance lines the typefaces on the edge of the bed—in white cotton sheets. She enters the bathroom. In the bathroom, she grips the oval, stainless steel bowl and turns the hot water spigot. When the water reaches ¾ full, she grabs a hand towel from the handle, turns the spigot to the left, and returns to the bed with the handheld items. She sits next to the bed and places the oval bowl on the bed and dips the towel into the bowl and wrenches it so that the towel acts as an oshibori. She begins to wash each typebar with the oshibori. Splotches of ink begin to occupy the towel's terrycloth composition. She places each typebar on the bed along its edge like an assembly line. When she places each typebar down, the typebar creates a darker halo around the typebars on the cotton sheet as the cotton sheet tries to absorb the water and the light weight of the typebars. She rubs the ink off the semicolon, colon, numbers, and quotation marks. When they are desiccated of their printed literary history, Valance assembles the washed typebars in the QWERTY panel as seen in the diagram on the other page (ignoring the typewheel) with the letters of the typebars turning toward her body so that she may see the letters protrude on the spring steel before her. Valance lets the air drink in the last microscopic water residue from the typebars and walks toward her drawers. She unrolls a 6 x 6 foot white Ingres sheet and walks the paper to the wall that faces the foot of the bed. She picks up the roll of white artist tape from the birch floor. With her left shoulder and lower torso holding the sheet to the wall, she begins to tear approximately seven pieces of tape (each four inches) and slabs them makeshiftingly to the Ingres. They hold the Ingres to the wall without her support. Then, she begins to tear one six foot tape from the artist roll four times and slowly tapes the Ingres along its edges and sides. She walks to her drawer and pulls out a colossal C-Thru Compass. Gripping the

knee-action bow compass, she walks back to the hung Ingres and circles the 0.5 mm mechanical pencil on the Ingres paper. Satisfied with the circular four foot diameter drawing on Ingres, she drops the compass on the floor, returns to her bed, undresses until she is nude, and lies down.

3

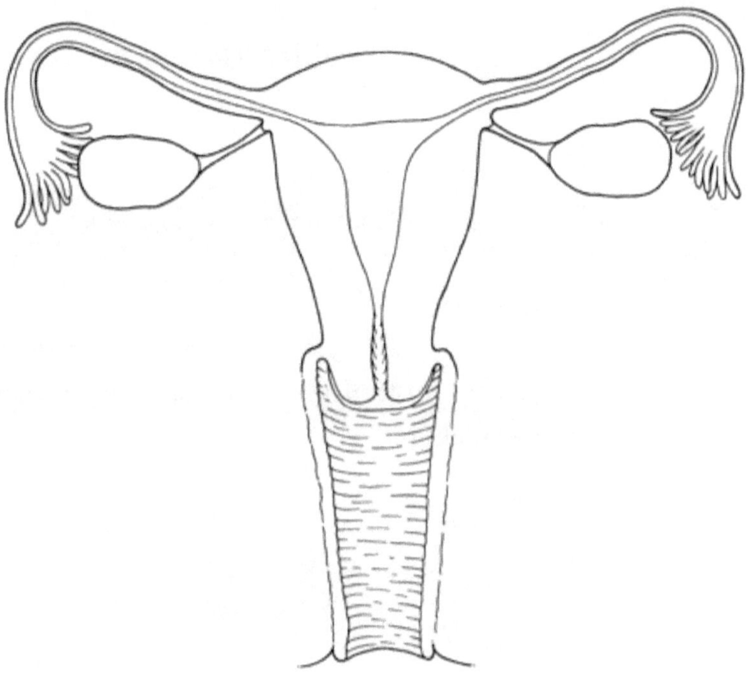

4 Ping Pong tournaments exist in some brothels in Thailand. These purse holders enter the entertainment facilities to exercise their purses' rights and act as participants in the ritual of human rights conflicts. Some have held chopsticks without hands and have been able to grab grapes, tofu, mango slices, and feed customers Pad Thai noodles regularly. A fancy type of fine dining and recreation of infertility. Valance is not a purse holder. She is a poet.

THE LAUNCH

SHUTTLE **e**: I've waited so long!
SHUTTLE **t**: We departed from the gate at 7:14 pm or 7:14 am. It was hard to tell. Day or night.
SHUTTLE **h**: There was a brief struggle.
SHUTTLE **e**: Oh, god, help me!

SHUTTLE **h**: Ahhhhhhhh, mother of God, Jesus Christ!
SHUTTLE **t**: How is everyone doing?
SHUTTLE **e**: NOOOOOOOOOOOO-OOOOOOOOOOO! (*Silent scream.*)

INT. SCENE – INGRES PAPER/MOON

We all landed on the INGRES MOON, the circular moon that Valance, our creator, drew before us, like so:

INT. SCENE – INTERIOR OF SHUTTLE **e, t,** and **h**

SHUTTLE **e**: I did not know when I took off. I did not come flying out of a large window of a 90-story building. I did not dive out of the gate as if I were launching off from the swimming pool diving board. A thump. A bounce. A thrust upward. I did not fling out of the windows as if I were a bullet pulled out of a revolver nor an arrow lifted off the face of the bow targeting the vanishing dot on the horizon. I did not hurl, leap, nor burst out of the open gate. We, Shuttle **t**, Shuttle **h**, and I did not uniformly ascend the clouds. We simply exited without arching my stiff back. I remember Shuttle **t** falling from me farther and farther. I couldn't see Shuttle **h** from my peripheral view. I remember the thick air, flying over the literary tapestries of forks and spoons. Some have looked at me hastily and have confused me with Hangul, the Korean alphabet. I was born in and am the fifth child in a family of 26 siblings. I remember being sinfully in the middle of the clan called Concatenation. I am a progeny of mixed marriages. My family tree sort of looks like this: Great-great-great grandparents belong to the Egyptian hieroglyph. And great-great grandparents were Phoenician. Great grandma and grandpa from Etruscan society. Grandma and grandpa from Greece, and now I am just an omelet of Roman mother and Cyrillic father.

SHUTTLE **t**: The cotton sheet was so warm then. When I entered the hole with the others, the world sort of collapsed. I missed basking under the florescent sun. It was warm and breathable then. I was lying on my side. There was so much open air. I know we all had to stay united. She told us that if we sacrificed ourselves for literature; for instance, like suicide bombers, that we would enter heaven and women would serve us carrying delicious plates of olives, paella, tuna crudo, with sesame beef tenon, yuzu, jalapeno! smoked aioli, (oh that smoked aïoli), mayonnaise, seasoned garlic, bacon wrapped rabbit and that brioche stuffing with fava beans and chanterelle madieira jus! Oh, I just couldn't take it. I would die if I missed such an opportunity. But it wasn't I who chose her. She chose us. We had no choice, but we had a choice. We were pretty much a confused bunch. Did I tell you she mentioned Alsatian onion tart: juniper balsamic, cambozola, black label, blue cheese? Have I mentioned that before? It seems so long ago when she revealed the first, second, and third prizes for our courage. We had courage then, lying on the cotton beach, gazing out into the cotton sea. We knew there was a world out there. I glanced while I was basking and glanced when I was launching and saw a man's goatee. I know someone was out there, watching out for us. Protecting our assets. This was what men do. Right? Protect our assets? Really, I am not an eater, but my, oh my, I hope it's worth it: fennel panisse, harissa sauce! My liver. Oh, my liver!

SHUTTLE **h**: Some of the debris that left my face thought I was a chair and sat on me. I did not like it at all. The nicest thing that ever sat on me was the wet cushion of the inkpad before flight. It was good to have my face macerated, though the maceration process was infinitesimally brief, and hardly worth mentioning. Earlier in my Semitic past, I had stood for a fence. I am now simply the non- archaic 8th child of modern Latin parents. Other authorities of my family's name have vulgarly addressed me as 'aha.' Please do not mistake me for an imbecile. There is a medley of Alexander the Great geographical conquest in me: I am a little bit Egyptian, a little bit Phoenician, a bit Greeky, a sample of Etruscan, and as you can see, I am a bit of a traveler. When she launched me from her base, I wasn't holding on to the patriotic flag: an emblem of all twenty-six members of my colored family. Armstrong wasn't an imbecile. This is where I was an imbecile.

Typewriter image from http://site.xavier.edu/polt/typewriters/tw-parts.html
Uterus diagram from http://holyoak.co/uterus-diagram-unlabeled.html

Three Poems

Shay Lawz

August

There is a plant in my room and a mirror above it. The plant sits atop a bookshelf and the mirror, small and red, hangs at eye level. The leaves, at their healthiest, touch the corner of the glass very softly. I have grown fond of the mirror, perhaps for its reflection of me. Perhaps for the way I see myself as flower —a growing thing. Over the phone my mother says, "You've got to water that *thing*, you hear me? Cut off the dead leaves."

wallpaper interlude

"   the house furnishes   images and a body
the same   " – Bachelard

A child is an open body.

Wallpaper is that which clothes the house is that which wears the child is that which sees.

I am a child and we are in the room with the mustard wallpaper and the photos grown like flowers on the wall. Grandma is a prettier version of her daughter, she will tell you this. She is not ashamed to say it; *no woman should ever be ashamed.* When she says this, it is my mother who she looks at. And it is through this image that I see another. Through this woman that I see another. When she says this, the glass slips out of her hand. And she does not say a word because it does not break, but I cry because it disappears and where does that leave me? A floor.

"I dreamed I was beautiful. I dreamed it and it felt real. I dreamed I was beautiful and the whole world smiled in my direction saying yes, yes, we're so glad you're here. Thank you for giving us something to look up to." – Yoko Ono

March

L tells me that her grandmother has died. I keep hold of the water. I see my grandmother in the mirror. I keep hold of the water. The plant dies. I keep hold of the water. I accept it. I keep hold of the water. I want to be home. I keep hold of the water. I want to be here. I keep hold of the water. I want here to be home. I keep hold of the water. I want to be home. I keep hold of the water.

The Dreams of Sedat Peker

Olivia Rose Walton

Sedat Peker demanded a sacrifice. He dreamed of blood, and I dreamed the dreams of Sedat Peker.

In January of 2016, when the snow fell so thick and deep we were locked into the apartment for a week, only leaving to fetch water, bread, and rolling papers, he makes an announcement directed at the Academics for Peace, who have signed a petition in response to the acute and specific violence of that year. Sedat Peker takes it upon himself to voice the concerns of the nation, regarding these restless and rebellious university professors. At the same time, he enters my dreams.

In that year, while a war in all but name is fought in the southeast, and while the cities endure their fair share of bombs, a year that could only be sated, as it happened, by a coup, this is what he says:

THE SO-CALLED INTELLECTUALS, THE BELLS WILL TOLL FOR YOU FIRST.

A message from Sedat Peker.

We will let your blood in streams and we will take a shower in your blood. If you ask my opinion,

> `you should not try to sink this STATE for your own health. The only reason that you are alive at the moment is the presence of the STATE and its survival. As I said in the aforementioned remarks, if the terrorists, you who are their supporters and foreign countries' intelligence services – in sum, all of you – accomplish your goals and turn this STATE into a nonfunctioning situation, you should well know that you will never be shown mercy by THE CHILDREN of this HOMELAND.`

I call the first dream the Delivery Boy Dream

A delivery boy pulled up on a scooter outside an apartment block in an indistinct suburb of the city—a *bakkal* on the corner, a *köfteci* across the street. Sedat Peker leaned over the balcony railing and rolled a Chesterfield between his fingers. I stood behind him. He had recently shaved the back of his neck. The boy below squinted up without getting off the scooter.

"We brought the blood, *beyefendi*."

Sedat Peker saw the boy's face as if it were right up in front of him. I, too, gazing over the man's shoulder, saw the face of the boy. A sesame seed rested on the side of the boy's mouth.

"What blood?" said the man.

The delivery boy had no time for this kind of thing. A delivery is a delivery.

"Sedat Bey, it is not my blood, all I know is that the box is marked *blood* and they told me to bring it to you."

"Who told you?"

"The men in the office in Mecidiyeköy."

Sedat Bey lit the cigarette.

"Give it to the doorman."

The boy unlocked the crate on the back of the scooter and lifted out a white refrigerated box. He passed this to a man standing just inside the shadow of the building. Then he made a gesture up at the balcony with his right hand, and drove off.

Sedat Peker allowed the cigarette to burn halfway before he took his first drag. From where we stood the city expanded and seemed to rush down to the sea. I saw it as he saw it. As is the way of dreams sometimes, the mind of the dream was his, was him. Not mine, not me. We shared the view, and the cigarette smoke, and the dream. The sea itself lay flat and indifferent, perhaps bored of the city. He too was bored, as he smoked.

The end of the cigarette came. He stubbed it out into a potted plant and thought about the blood. He had stood on a podium; people surrounded him, waving red flags and calling for that very blood, or maybe any blood, he was never sure they even knew. Of the few things that mattered, this was not one of them. The blood in him rose up to meet the people and he cried out, giving them the words that softened their taut throats and caused them to push their hands up even higher into the air.

They shouted, he shouted. He said, "Their blood will run freely on our streets."

"He who speaks of peace during wartime is as much a traitor as he who speaks of war during peacetime," the former interior minister had once said.

The colours of the day began to press on him. The city's walls, all of its walls, grew heavy and threatened to push down into the earth, pulling with them all the carpets, hanging pictures, cabinets, fridges, couches, lovers, samovars, house slippers, disquieted housewives, dogs, televisions, sausages, and bags of sugar held within the walls. All of it would sink into the earth and the sea and there he would stand, the only one to have recognised that this was what was coming and to have relished it.

This was why he was bored.

The presence of the blood downstairs annoyed him. The smell of blood made him feel ill and he avoided it. Besides, to shower in blood would cause a great mess, and the scent would linger. He could, he reasoned, stay with his mistress until the smell faded. That thought pleased him. But how would he get the blood to come out in a shower? Should he bathe in it? It is important to follow through with one's promises. He had said shower. "I will take a shower in your blood." Ah, fuck. He went inside and down the stairs, passing a sleeping woman and me on the way there.

In the shadow of the doorway the doorman stood. Light from outside fell at his feet.

"Sedat Bey, *selam aleyküm*."

"*Aleikum Aleyküm selam*."

"Here it is. Where shall I put it?"

The man paused. He pulled another Chesterfield and this time he turned to look at me. The dream got louder.

"How do I know that this is the correct blood?"

He looked me in the eye.

The doorman answered.

"How can I know?"

Sedat Peker turned away from me. He said only, "Ah."

Blood is blood. The origin of the blood is by now besides the point. It could be ox blood, or horse blood. He looked at the box in the doorman's hands. It had a delivery note taped to it. At the top was a crest. The Ministry of Justice. So, real blood then.

Satisfied he said, "Yes." And then, "Put it in the fridge."

The dream ends.

In the waking evening, after a hot day, we listen to Marvin Pontiac with the windows open. *I'm a doggy, and I'm naked almost all the time.* The *turunç* tree beyond the window is heavy with fruit. The fruit in turn are heavy with snow. My soft-eyed friend paces with strides that are not soft at all. He's reading. I'm rolling a joint over the pages of my open book.

I say, "Can I read this to you?"

He says, "Sure. Go ahead."

It's from *Ka*, by Roberto Calasso.

I read.

> When Śiva wiped out the world, all combinations of existence would flow within him, without needing to exist. The mind and the outside were not separate entities – perhaps not even entities at all. Penetrating each other, they lost all their shyness. The stream was one. The dreadful and the delicate surfaced together, in pairs, indifferent to each other, like distant relatives. Then they bid each other goodbye. Immediately something else took their place. An incessant migration. All forms, all forces: they were Śiva's herd. That's why they call him Paśupati, Lord of the Herds.[1]

My friend rises and walks to the window, opens it and leans out to look at the *turunç* tree. I put the book down and shut my eyes. Soon I am asleep, but I can hear him speak even as I disappear.

---

1 Calasso, Robert. *Ka*, (Vintage, 1999), p. 121

So began the second dream of Sedat Peker. I call this one The Seer.

I am in the kitchen. He comes in. He says, "Make me eggs with *sucuk*." I reach for a frying pan. This time, we are separate. He has come to visit me. He sits on a chair where he can see me work and begins to speak.

"Knowingly or not, I have a role to play in your life. And *role* is an apt word for it: you believe that you are the central actor in your life, and yet if there was an audience who watched your caprices and your turmoil from comfortable seats at a safe distance from all the spitting and crying, they'd be able to talk amongst themselves after the show and say. Well, she was great, you know, really convincing, but of course the thing is that she didn't understand anything at all. I suppose it's a metaphor for modernity, they'd say, What with that character lurking around behind her all the time conducting her affairs without her knowing it, she really has no say in much at all though she believes she does. Such is our condition, they would say, And we shall not know the culprits until we know ourselves. Let's have a drink on the terrace, they will say."

I crack eggs into the pan, over and over. Thirty eggs pass between my fingers, fifty, a hundred, and none sticks. They slide from the pan, onto the floor and out the window. The man goes on.

"Character is a misleading word for me. I'm not a mere character – like you I'm a person, and I've a name and a family. There are state files recording my movements and the names of my parents, my religion, the hospital where I was born, whether or not I've done my military service. (I have.) I am cemented in reality. I even pay taxes. The difference is that I know what is going to happen and I've decided to prepare for it, whereas you think you have some idea – or you don't care – but it's neither here nor there what that idea is. I've never stopped working; you sit and take photographs of yourself, to share or to delete, obsessed as you are with a fairly limited range of concerns. It's not even that I'm watching you all the time – I don't need to, you do it for me. Everything you do is so well recorded that for a while I became suspicious that you'd caught on to what is happening to you, but then I realised it could not be so. How charming you are, how free of true deceit. Of course to those around you, you're a liar and a flirt, a cheat at cards, a desirable conceit, not a real person but an artful representation of one.

"Wait – perhaps I have underestimated you. You have causes, and lovers. What you lack is the long vision of things, and the will not just to plan for them but to form them. I saw it coming, all of this, and shaped myself as I needed to in order to be prepared. You really do like to look at yourself in the mirror. You also look at photographs of people that you love or have loved. I understand that you read certain serious books. I see also that you have recently developed a taste for blood sports. You also read and watch the news, in order to keep abreast of developments. Is that enough? Sometimes you even read about me. Did you see my videos?

"You did, didn't you. You enjoyed them. There was that one with clips of me making speeches about the Chief – I mean, when in history has an uneducated boy from the sticks, from the back quarters of the city, from the hard but living streets, become the powerful and beloved leader of a nation that bends to his iron hammer as hot metal bends to the hands of a smith? Never? No, many times. Oh, but it's an old story. We knew our turn would come. The question remains as to what happens next. But I do not speak of this. I think about it, and I make notes.

"Of course most things seem to us – here I put you and I, as humans, in the same category – to be special. In fact they are not, or not in any fundamental way. You were recounting that to friends just the other day. Yes, it was me you saw there. Someone had told you, Repetition is very important, and you remembered that."

I slice the *sucuk*. While I slice it, I begin to speak. Pieces of *sucuk* collect at my feet like my own hair. My hair begins to fall too. A dog with a head hewn from stone eats the sausage, one piece at a time.

"In the 1950s there was the boy from Aydınlı. His name was Menderes."

"Yes, go on."

"He came along with the vote of the peasants, ready to build roads and offer the people freedoms they had been denied."

"He did, indeed."

"The former he succeeded in."

"Thank you, America. Thank you, Marshall Plan."

"But by 1961 Menderes had been executed and his government overthrown."

"You're interested in that, aren't you."

"I am interested in patterns. Repetition is important."

"Repetition lies."

"Now the pattern is like this. A party comes in on the promise of reform but sets to work in secret separating the population into two categories, the People, and the Elite. Tensions rise. The party makes sure everybody has an enemy."

"And then what?"

"And then there is a coup. Like clockwork, every ten years. Give or take. And it all begins again."

"Which is why you said to your friends, It's just one fucking thing after another."

"It's not my line."

"One fucking thing after another."

Now the dog rests its head on his leg. Sedat Peker points at my chest as he speaks.

"You do this, you read, you write, you follow things, every day there is something new, but nothing changes. And you can't see how it all works anyway. It's sweet because you're a bit drunk from rakı and swimming in the sun for so long. Your friends nod and laugh, they agree, they're also just about at the point of ducking out of all this, the world we were raised to believe was ours. (I was right, you were wrong). The girl opposite you talks about getting some goats on a farm, and you offer to look after them while she works in the big hospital in the city. You do this because you are in love with her. There is more drink, and you make fun of a woman who is standing in the water wearing a head-to-toe pink swimsuit made of the same stuff as men's swim shorts. The tall girl says, If you don't want to see naked people, then just don't come here.

"You like to be on that girl's side and so you agree. But you probably feel bad for making fun of her. You think, How petty is God? Would he punish you, for mocking a woman who covers herself even while she swims? If that woman's God is real, and he rules you too, what will he take from you? What is it you are ashamed of? Is shame your God? Your tall friend has no such concerns; she makes no bargains with spectres. Drunk and stupid in the sun, and thinking about God, you catch sight of me, don't you, in the pines behind the little hut where a woman is making fried zucchini flowers to serve to you with yoghurt.

"I do follow you."

He keeps speaking. I slice and I listen. The dog watches me and does not blink.

I wake. I am on the couch, and a man is standing in the room in the dark speaking to me. He is a man I know. I am awake. This man, the waking man, paces as he talks. My hands are folded over a pack of cigarettes. My clothes are on the floor.

"Well I mean life is just one fucking thing after another, isn't it? You read about Śiva, and all the other gods. It seems to me also that you'd be able to grasp the fundamental thing about those gods – they're not gods the way the people chanting *Allahu akbar* or fantasizing about the Pope would expect. *Those* gods are all-powerful and omnipresent, waiting in the shadows of everything and with one eye on the clock at all times. Doomsday is always approaching, the whip and the balm always in the same hands. These gods – the ones you and I grew up with, gods who originated in the sacred red parts of the world – see no limit to their powers, and we are expected to behave accordingly. We are expected to be contrite. They are not 'they' at all but He, just the one, and it is not enough – or maybe it is, I don't know, I feel fucked when I think about it."

Sedat Peker sits on the couch now. The sausages and the eggs and the dog are gone. He answers my friend.

"You are right to be fed up with that type of god, given what has taken place here. No doubt this is why you are drawn to the gods this girl is reading about, Indra and Śiva and so on. I myself find them useful models, too. As one of the *brahman* explains, these gods may be gods alright but they're as vain and petty as men – though they use men to achieve their own ends. Man thus has some of the nobility of the workhorse. Man is tamed and useful, a little dumb. The gods are capricious, they leap around the world forming its mountains and its myths with their escapades. They make love and pursue underage women; they seduce and destroy kings, and kill themselves for love and desire. To them the world is a casino.

"The world of domesticated animals is the world of men; the world of wild animals is the world of the gods. But as you will see from this comparison they are nonetheless driven by instinct, which some would call base by definition. They seek out things that you or your friends seek out too: love and sex, the bodies of others, sweet food and cool water in the summer, a home, blood. They are grand because they are the gods, they emanate from the origins of Time and Matter, and so their stories become myths and archetypes by which men are desperate to live. Yet they discover little that they were not born with."

My friend stops pacing to squat in front of me. He touches my face.

"Then what do we know?"

"What?"

"Wake up. You always fall asleep. What did you say?"

"I saw Sedat Peker in my dream, and he was telling us something."

"Ya? What was it?"

I roll over, sit up and light a cigarette.

"You want to know? He said something like this. 'It is the Seer, the one who does nothing but observe the force of life that dwells within him and all things, who comes closest to power.'"

He takes my feet in his hands. I put my hands around his face. I speak the last words of Sedat Peker.

"Yet here again power is not what you or I was raised to believe it to be. It's not the ability to strike down the enemy or force your will on the nation. Power here is knowledge of the fundamental truth of the universe. It is harmony of the opposites that both observe and constitute each other: the mind, and the self that watches it. The Seers were the ones who approached this kind of force. It is them I wish to emulate. I carry the gods in my pocket to remind myself that they are not the limits of possibility."

"I hope he dies."

"He will."

The third dream is called Chickpeas.

I am on an island. It's a tropical island, and F-16s fly past overhead. My father is sometimes with me on this island, helping us, the guerrillas, with engineering works. He is there this time, pointing to a gash in the land where the earth needs to be cleared. Next to him is a man in a white shirt like a waiter carrying a big metal dish, more like a tray. His mouth is a gash like the one in the earth. He would bow low if I told him to. There is something weak in his face. Is he a supplicant now? With confused eyes he calls at me, offering me the food that he carries on his tray. He wants to help the war effort. The tray is full of chickpeas cooked in tomato sauce. He has a table now, and some plastic bowls. Here, here, eat, he says. He is Sedat Peker. He hands me a dish of chickpeas in tomato sauce, and walks on with his tray.

pinto
("chick" and slang for "penis" in brazilian portuguese)

Lucas de Lima

pinto ("penis" & slang for "chick" in brazilian portuguese)

if the dream is to go beyond empire

if the dream is to stretch our extremities

all the way thru

if o poder emana do povo

& the people's emanations

refuse to be privatized

what does it mean that i fisted pinto

& became a chicken

what does it mean that pinto opened my hole

without extracting my soul

Malvina Sammarone: Communicating The Incommunicable

Aster(ix) Journal

Malvina Sammarone uses both of her hands in her drawings, creating a reversed mirrored image. The action itself can be perceived as an extreme act, exhausting the mental and physical. While looking at her drawings we lose the focal point and start to perceive what stays in the periphery, on the edges. This is one of the many reasons we are featuring her work in this issue. As a visual artist she transits through drawing, photography, video, and installations, where time, duration, unpredictability, chance, repetition, and process permeate all her works. She's based in São Paulo, Brazil.

Aster(ix): In your work, drawing seems to be the core of your activity and the source of your creativity. We want to ask you what distinguishes drawing for you from other disciplines such as painting, etc. Why do you choose drawing as your main tool of expression?

Malvina Sammarone: I think in part this happens because I've always identified myself with the line, traces, sketches as a tool of expression and another because of architecture, which I also studied.

Aster(ix): When did you start making art?

MS: I started very young taking classes of drawing and watercolor. Later when I went to the University (Industrial Design and then, Architecture) I would attend drawing and painting classes in artists' studios. After my BA, I worked with a landscape architect for a while. But I was always producing art. In the beginning of the 90s I decided to work just as a visual artist.

Aster(ix): In this issue, we are thinking about edges. Aesthetic edges, political, emotional, etc. In what ways are you interested in your process to push against edges, if at all?

MS: I've been thinking a lot about how I could approach certain political issues, For example, violence against children and young people in my country. Domestic violence against women, children and the elderly. Differences in identity... maybe in my photography and video work, however I do not usually exhibit those because unfortunately there are not enough opportunities in São Paulo. But in my work I do touch on issues of edges, memory and loss.

Aster(ix): Your drawings have a strong performative connotation, can you tell us what is the role of time and duration in your work? When do you know a drawing is finished?

MS: Time and duration are very present in my work, as well as the notion of possibility and unpredictability, error and exhaustion. These are incorporated in my artistic process by using the possibilities and limitations of the body.

And this, the body, as a measurement tool to register geometries, figures, numbers, through the movement, will be executed for as long as consciousness flows in a continuous and indefinite period. The longer the action lasts, the more changes physically and psychologically, perception and reality become different. If a transformation happens, one can decide to change the action or complete it.

Aster(ix): In your process it seems like you use rules, physical constrictions and repetitions in order to perform your drawing. Why do you use this strategy and in which way does this modality affect your work? How does your process work?

MS: Yes, I give myself 'instructions'. Sometimes I exploit repetitive movements, with mental statements. For example: How will lines occupy paper space? Occasionally, I apply a rule, as orders of reverse movements, stipulated as a priori. The drawings are configured as traces left by the graphite deposit on the surface of paper, a record/trait of mental versus physical activity. Also I will use rubber bands on my arms to constrict my movements. I have another series of works called *Numbers*, where the materials I use varied papers and permanent pen. It is a numerical sequence that is being done exhaustively, without ending. The work is bound to the limits of the body and time.

Aster(ix): What and who are your influences?

MS: I have many. For example the minimal/post-minimal/conceptual artist Sol LeWitt. He is an artist who is interested in ideas, elementary forms, modularity, grids, repetition, serialism, systems and instructions. The fact that collaborations were part of his creative process. I also use Eva Hesse as a reference, for her search for the authentic, the appropriation of unexpected materials, and the appropriation of serial and modular forms in the production of variable and disturbing works. Other artists such as Hanne Darboven, Bruce Nauman, Vito Acconci Tacita Dean, Susan Hiller, Francis Alys, Richard Long, Trisha Brown, Lygia Clark, Helio Oiticica, Nelson Felix are great influences.

I also look to literature. Samuel Beckett interests me because of his circular form of reasoning, extracting something from nothing, and communicating the incommunicable. Julio Cortazars work provokes me as a reader, because of its attempt to put a man within his limits, and at the same time, a playful exercise. Other writers include, Jorge Luis Borges, Italo Calvino, Clarice Lispector, Georges Didi-Huberman, Giles Deleuze.

And then there is music. For me John Cage is one of the most innovative experimenters in the field of music and art. Brian Eno: The work of the "non-musician", as Eno describes himself, interests me since the 80's, when I became in contact with his experimental and ambient electronic music and his collaborations with so many other artists. And there is always Classical Music.

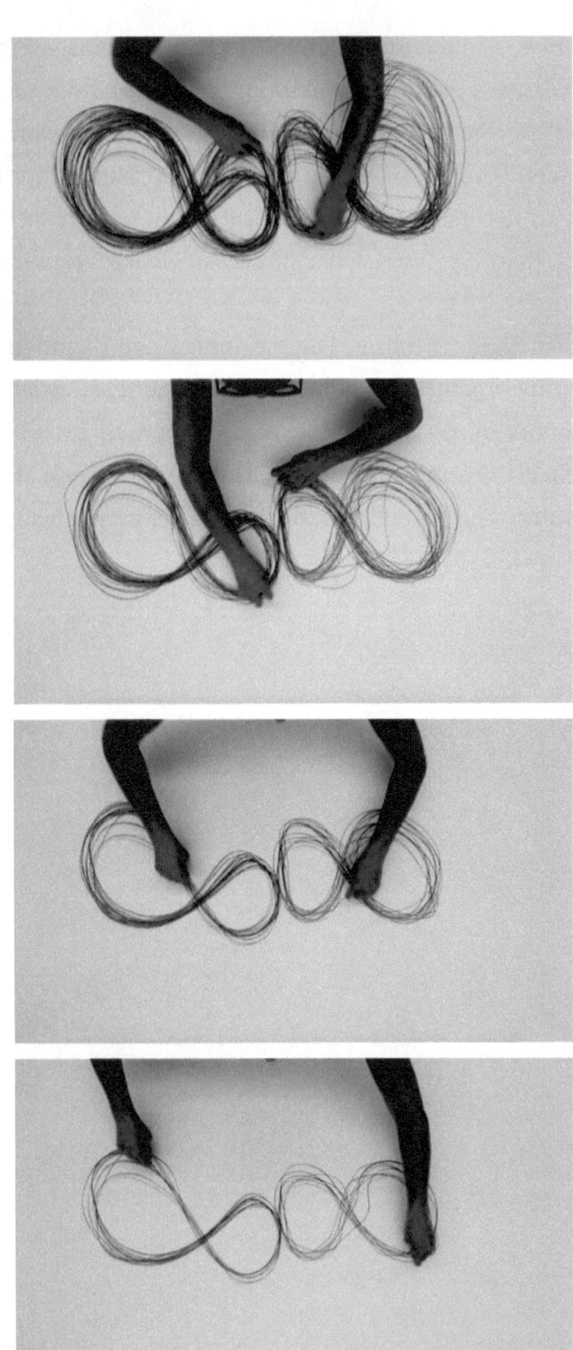

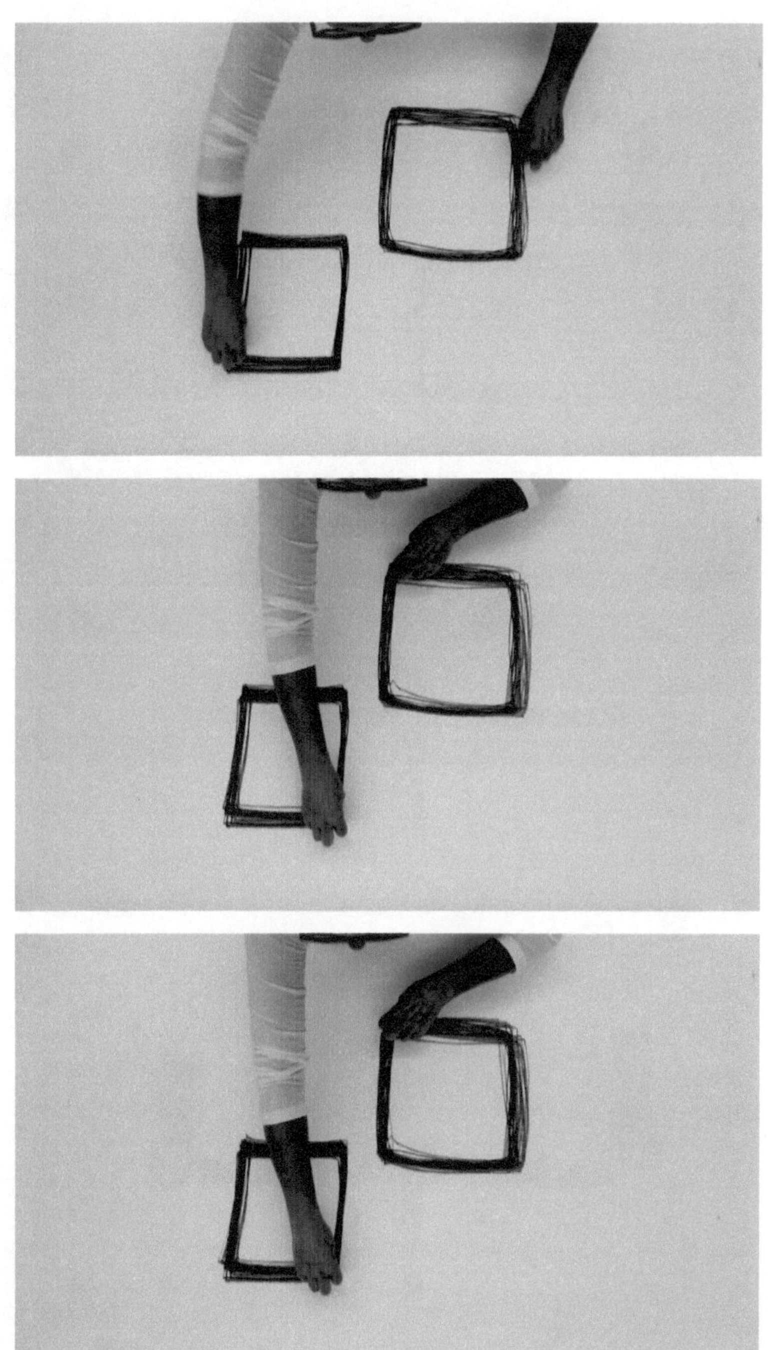

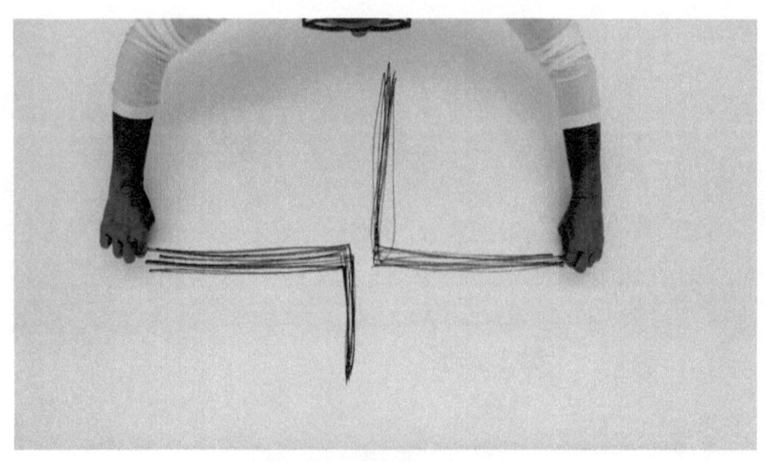

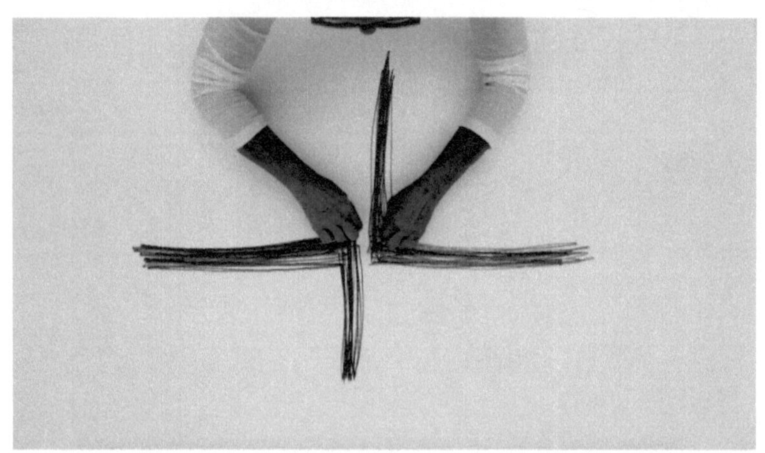

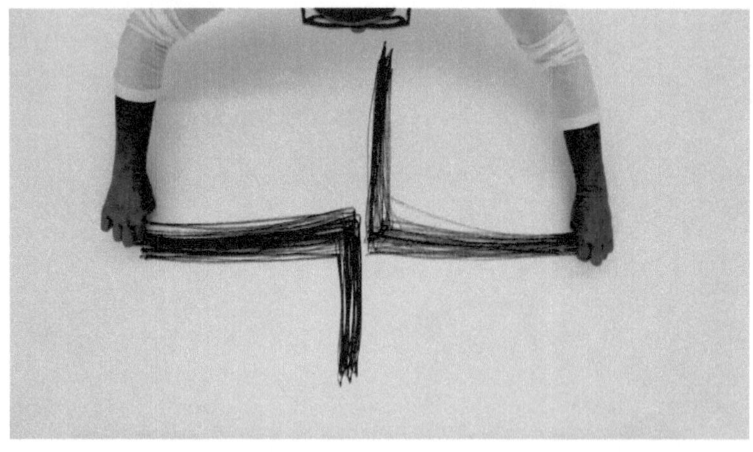

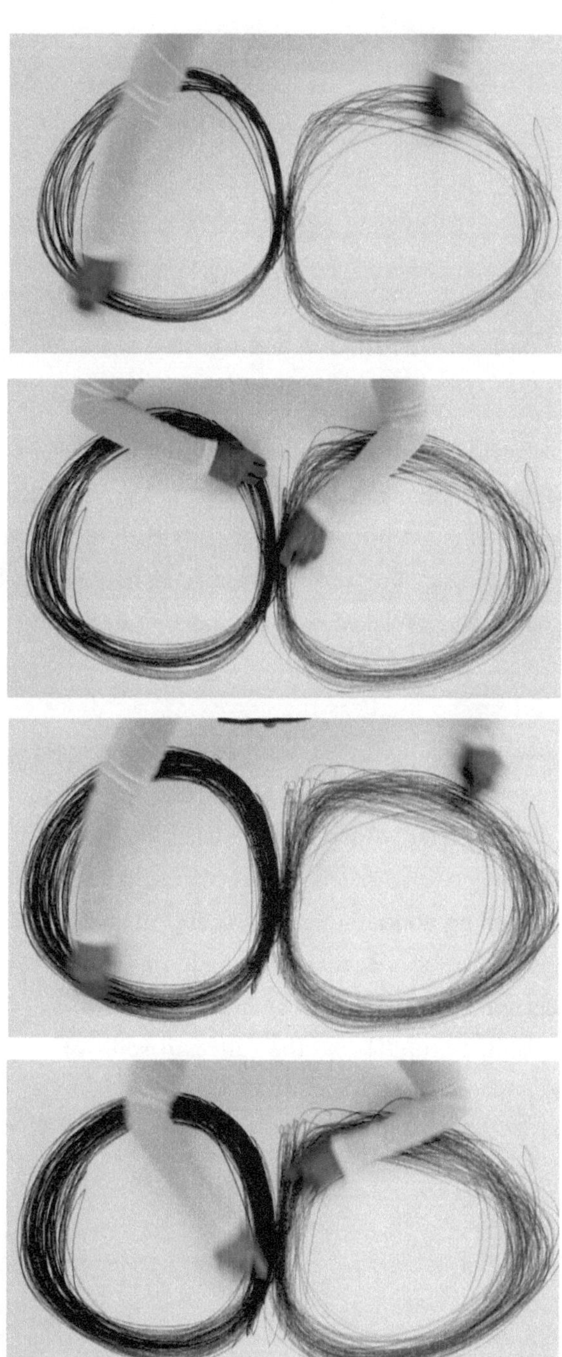

that I eat birds/

Nicole Callihan

and even dreamed last night/ I had coughed the feathers up/ at the breakfast table/and Ella said/ daddy doesn't eat birds/ and I said/ I know/ daddy doesn't eat birds/ but that I have seen him/ standing by a bush/ hovering over two/ and I myself have been in his hand/ and leoninely loving/ he has licked me/ behind my ears/ that I eat pig for breakfast/ not unlike the pig/ Suzanne got the boys/ for Christmas/ but dead/ and not so loud/ as the graveyard/ we drove by/ to get to their house/ to see the pig/ in a crate/ god it was so grey/ in Missouri/ I thought/ everyone probably wanted to die/ that maybe I prefer fish/ but it makes a thermometer/ of my blood/ that I like things/ in wrappers/ that turn my fingers orange/ that I have already eaten/ but for some reason/ I am talking about hunger/ because hunger/ is elliptical/ like love/ or good correspondence/ that the plums/ are actually on the counter/ because I don't like biting/ into cold fruit/ with my teeth/ I like it room temperature/ I like the split and spill/ of spoiled things/ before they spoil

Soft Bodies

Nicole Callihan

While sweeping the carcasses of ladybugs into a blue dust pail, I think of how it might be a good idea to build soft bodies around robots, or of how I might use my own soft body to surround a good, patient robot who has only mechanical desires. I could donate the flesh of my thighs and the pulp of my lungs, and seeing this robot on the street, you might think she is me, and maybe you would speed up because you remember that terrible thing I did three falls ago, or maybe you would slow down, because, twice, I was nice at drop-off. I would like to feel oil slowly poured into my ear. My student says that if we can offer robots to the ill and infirm no one will have bed sores, and my Facebook feed says that my dad's stepmother died several days ago, and yesterday, taking Eva for braces, I thought it would be easier if her teeth were constructed out of manmade materials and would, thus, already be straight. There are buttons on my back which can be pressed to make me audibly moan. For what I am hardwired, I cannot say.

Room for Rent

Nicole Callihan

I am looking to fill a room this winter. The window frames the window's frame, and, right now, there is snow falling, though, of course, by the time you read this and email me and look for the keys that let you in wherever you already live and spit-comb your brows and find your scarf and wait for the train and get on the train and read whatever dog-eared volume of poetry you happen to have in your bag and turn away once, hearing a voice that sounds an awful lot like a voice you thought you had forgotten, and then turn back to the poems, but with more longing, the snow will have stopped. It always stops; it always starts again. In this way, it is like geraniums. I eat white foods from white bowls and fear some things more than others. Also, there are tens of light switches along my walls, and sometimes I cannot find them. I hope that this will not dissuade you. Small pets are welcome. I once carried a baby bird for so long in a flannel I didn't even realize it had died.

The disquiet of being Anonymous

Andrea Jeftanovic

Translated by J. C. Reyes
from Andrea Jeftanovic's *Don't Accept Candy from Strangers*

Every time the full moon shines, we blow off our friends, postpone our appointments. You always wait beneath the splendor of the night. I finally understood as much after weeks of watching your window. When you reappeared one Sunday much like the day we first met, before my astonished face, you pointed to the plethoric moon like you were holding a balloon. I assumed rightly that these things could only happen in overcrowded cities like this one, where people's homes verged into other people's homes. I carry our record of elapsed time on the calendar hanging from my kitchen door.

Like every Sunday, we see each other after our rounds, our jogging, our trying to read and then abandoning the same book, our many times opening and closing the refrigerator door, until you appear like a mirage in front of my apartment. There have been many times when I've thought to myself it would be our last encounter, but in the end, you're always waiting for me playing out the same scene. There have been times when I've wanted to stop altogether, but I can't seem to imagine something more important to do. I don't know if it was the curtains left open neglectfully, the encounter after our own respective showers. You, with a towel wrapped to your armpits and a black dress splayed on the bed. Me, covered to the waist, my jogging shoes paraded on the floor. Surely, we both thought about drawing the curtains, but something held us back. We stood there paralyzed, watching each other steadily. That night's darkness sliced by bedroom lights. A considerable time passed. I didn't know what to do as you moved your lips into a cryptic appeal.

In a sharp wave, you strip off the towel, take one step forward, get to within an inch of the window. Before anything else, we acknowledge each other. Your body forested in lines, stuck in light and shadow. From a distance, your body is ablaze. It's uncomfortable feeling that you're exploring, that you're trying, same as I am, to memorize shapes and patterns. I study your dimensions, the color of your skin, your figure and depth. We roam over our faces, at first crossing fingers over eyelids, sliding them along noses, up and combing eyebrows, down and undoing our lips. Sketching ovals around them, probing cheekbones, coming full circle at our chin. Drowning our hands in hair, combing from our roots, pausing to swirl and swirl at the nape. We close our eyes, open our lips. Massage our neck, relax our muscles, pinch our earlobes. Fingertips traveling down our sternum, tracing backward along an imaginary neckline. You start diffusing before my eyes, I try focusing once and then twice and watch your figure bend. A minute-long truce. You bring an index finger to your mouth, draw a halo with your salivated fingertips, trace a humid path around your breasts. I am one step behind, doing the same. I fantasize from a distance about your stiff nipples. I imagine all our neighbors paralyzed, watching us as they lean forward at their window sills, gazing at us from those black boxes embedded in such long and narrow buildings. My body thickens, I bury my fingers into my ribs until it hurts. With my arms crossed, I trim my waist. Later, you sit on the carpet, serenely exploring the soles of your feet. I keep up with you. Making circles around your ankles, quickly and intensely riding up your legs. And now up on your feet.

You turn around. I straighten my spine as you do yours; a scar divides your back. Is it a hernia? You turn just when I'm about to abandon you. I turn around, open-mouthed, and I regain my senses the moment I recognize again the color on the wall. I miss the traffic, the street noise, and wonder if everyone's died, if we've survived some catastrophe.

The glass gets patchy, each window pane left in circles of mist. You command me, with the back of your hand, to soften, and as always, I obey. We stretch our bodies, and I feel like we're going to flood the windows soon if this doesn't end. I can't manage to ask you about the night's silence when, suddenly, you let your hand fall quickly from forehead to bellybutton like a grand brushstroke. I just want to curl up and hold myself. But you punish me with your dilated time.

At this point, I start wondering about our neighbors touching themselves in the silence of their own darkness, devising for themselves some appropriate ritual. Denying the following day they'd spied on this scene, all this just a dream between their pillow and the sheets. You bring me back to you when you insinuate avenues through your muscles. You reproach me with a glance, I continue. Your fingers indiscernible, my hands uncovered. I adjust my breathing so you don't hear it. Your fingers each time more inconspicuous. My hands exposed by mechanical movements. From such a distance, we get closer. Our bodies attuning our wavy cracks, our recessions and peaks. In a spasm, we replay our entire childhoods. Your nameless pupils rescue me from the wish to throw myself into the lower stories. To get up and fall to my knees in some faraway country. Something brings us together in the void, something tries to drag us into oblivion. Someone turns the lights on and then off. Applause. And then the same glowing solitude. Each person to their bedroom, resuming their distances, leaving a circular stain on the carpet. For a moment, I thought I'd spooned your body into mine, felt your shape in mine. More applause, there's an extended standing ovation. Many times I've been to the point of some ridiculous curtsey, but we sustain each other by the same smirk. Your lips approach the glass, and I approach with mine; we give each other a goodbye kiss.

After you leave, I notice the uneven buildings, the neighboring elderly couple watching a television show of raucous colors from their couch, one and another passerby walking along the plaza that separates our buildings, a chimney that trims the clouds, the tidy roof tiles of a house. Between one encounter and the other, I spy your windows always closed and with thick curtains. One night I notice two people in distinct apartments as two lights shut off almost simultaneously. Your balcony plants look well-kempt, though I've never figured out when and by whom they're watered. One afternoon I thought I saw a boy, his small shadow moving restlessly from one side to the other and I managed to see an explosive forelock. Could it be your son? A nephew? The more I try to glimpse details of the home I can't tell if you have two nightstands, each for a different purpose, a man's clothes hanging over the back of a chair. I'm intrigued by the small movements throughout the day. Might you live here? Is it an apartment you occupy only on special occasions?

For the next encounter, you smoked, you flicked a lighter that sparked like a makeshift fire. A breath you later exhaled in puffs that submerged you in clouds. A camera flash sounded, and we remained intact, the terrace as it was. Had someone taken a picture of us? You tilting your head toward the ashtray at the center of the table. Me closing my eyes and imagining a hand over my shoulder searching blindly for me. Suddenly, we looked at the same window, where our lawyer neighbor was hanging his jacket on across the back of his Viennese chair, which he did every afternoon, later collapsing on the white couch. His body tired, his countenance completely shut off. I don't want to age like him, though I do stay attuned to his evening sorrows, to the effects of those defeats that plunge him into the cushions. These neighbors who exist because of all the precarious construction nearby. At night the open windows compelled you to share in the echo of the clanging argument racing down the hall, of the wall-drilling that ended and then restarted, of the neighbors' faces host to flaws and pockmarks that don't belong to them, it was the woman with the wide brim hat who returned her keys and walked away dragging a suitcase, on the first floor, her hand on a knee that wasn't her husband's, her voice graver than the upstairs schizophrenic who screeches until his sleeping pill kicks in. On the lower building rooftops, there are invalid animals, capable of surviving for survival's sake, that dig up trash and hunt for insects. I keep looking at the city's other extreme, statues and plazas, apartments with slate rooftops, stork nests, bat nests, (should I go on?), a terrace where we can distinguish between an aproned maid and a woman sitting with dark sunglasses holding a tray. I turn on the headboard lamp and the whole suite lights up, not like the kitchen that exists only in fragments before the whole thing comes into view.

There are moments I find myself skeptical about your return. And then I hear the dog's footsteps two floors up, the keys whispering just outside, the grazing of a rope that drives diagonally like the wind, a swinging rusted wire. I recognize the door latch sound of the woman next door, the maladjusted table board. I go downstairs, I guess whose steps might be on the landing, it's the prim, educated man, I ask him for the time despite the clock on the wall.

"Twenty-five to nine."

You should already be at the window. You point to your watch, insist twenty minutes to nine like a reprimand. Have you said something? Are you alone? Only the soft rumbling of the traffic outside. "Do you have a new scar on your lower back? What happened between your back and glutes? A serious illness or childhood accident? Something minor? Recently or far back?" I'm puzzled by the question I baited before I could bite my tongue. Truth is we've never dared ask each other anything from the balcony. I don't know your name or age, what you do or how you smell. I know that we pay the same in building fees, that our telephone numbers start with the same trio of digits, I also know that you belong to me, that you exist once a month, and that it's that or nothing. So if one day I wait for you outside or I call you, even though I don't know the number (I'd only be able to dial those first three digits and stand there with a dead tone), or I write you something without knowing what name to address the envelope to, you're liable to abandon this scene and retreat from the stage forever. I knew it that time, when I sensed it had been something special, unique; and so I started making a desperate show and you drew the curtains so briskly that it pains me even to remember it. I was stuck there, on my feet, alone and naked, with my body trembling and my hands rehearsing some useless gesture, imagining the neighbors were laughing hysterically, that I was some surreal impression of a person in the heart of the city. Which is why I now control myself, settle for your body like a movie screen, for that two-dimensional fantasy. I wait for that Sunday, to feel myself too far inside each and every meter that separates us, to hear the neighbors applaud, get intoxicated with dizziness. To go to bed alone with that absent French kiss, empty of flavor, counting the stories to your apartment, crossing out the days on the calendar.

You are, I am. The concierge's son, who sometimes offers me the ball when I come in, plays soccer against the wall. That night we went over our scene like so many before it, when suddenly we noticed a body falling; a neighbor had leapt into the void, a thick seizure on the horizon, a body falling, falling, piercing the apartments below us,

The eleventh,

Tenth,

Ninth,

Eighth,

Third,

Second.

The first floor was the crash of his body against the ground, shouts. We hesitated, your mouth flapped open, you were slow to comprehend that to your right, to your left, everybody was screaming at the same pitch to where you couldn't discern your scream from everybody else's. You went to the far end of the bedroom, we had to dress quickly and rush downstairs, I needed your arms in that terrible moment, I focused, I didn't want to lose my head, or waver, or disaffect myself, you have to be there, I looked for you in the mob that had crowded the entrance, neighbors in pajamas, walking awkwardly in their slippers, others with their flies poorly zipped, the concierge laying a wool blanket on the body, the ambulance siren, the paramedics making their way through, neighbors forming a second circle, me peering across the women. You have to be here, I should recognize you, if you really are mine, I look for your auburn hair, your small frame, more neighbors approach, the fireman demands a way through, the human flock disperses, the neighbors conjecture psychological trouble, heartbreaks, aberrant indications of something as he took out the trash, as he took the elevator, because who after all is not a stranger to anonymity. I smiled at some girl who looked at me spitefully probably thinking I was trying to seduce her, later I made a gesture to a woman that seemed too old to be you and she ignored me, I can't scream a name, stop everything and shout for the neighbor who meets me under the full moon. All of us witnesses to a nosedive.

When they removed the body and everybody returned to their apartments, I also went upstairs. Your window was in total darkness, and you might have been running to the exit, leaving me precisely when I needed you to tend to my sheets, change the pillow, change my position, me, with my mouth pressed to my knees curled up in a home I imagined, because ultimately only the lawyer neighbor exists, the police, the firemen, perhaps one kiss under a street light, a lantern looking for you, me at the window observing nada, the pain tearing the neighbors from the disquiet of being anonymous to each other, faces that resign themselves, eyebrows that bend helplessly, one to the right and the other obliquely, registers of a shared tragedy.

A body nosedives,
not from the sixth floor,
not from the third,
not from the second,
not from the eleventh,
but from the twelfth.

Not an accident, or perhaps a deliberate one, despite how incompatible that is, flying into the everything and nothing, tenants having supper without anybody sounding the alarm for what was about to come, not even a goodbye, a curiosity, a surprise, just dead murmurs. There are living rooms pleading, lights on low, jumps predisposed to everything but happiness, with splattered blood, a decision that tips over like a glass cup, a purring anxiety before the final hour, before the mid-hour. A body now like a constellation on the asphalt that has nothing organic anymore. A human installation at the center of meteors and planets that grazed its fall.

The calendar that's knotted to the clock has arrived: twenty minutes to nine. You are, I am. My body doesn't react, I don't get excited anymore, I feel inert inside and out. Something gives me the feeling that this reenactment is going to be our last, I stop the blinds at the point of shutting when my desolate mouth announces there will be no more games. Not exactly a restlessness, something else, a cold chest, hot and frozen, my legs icy, my hands frosted. My eyes temperate, empty. Empty eyes inevitably go stern or, if not stern because they're empty, no matter how fixed, go huge. I refuse to wake up again from viscous dreams without so much as being able to pronounce a name, some random arrangement of letters, some disarray of sound. It doesn't matter anymore whether the stage is set or the theater is absent of spectators, whether neighbors offer a standing ovation at their armchairs or brusquely shut their curtains. I simply retire to bed or I give up, whatever you want, my body doesn't respond, it just can't anymore. I draw the curtains shut and sit at my bed, I hold my head in my hands for a while, later I shrink into myself. I pass several long minutes keeled over, when the bell interrupts me, my apartment doorbell. I open the door not to leave but to let you in,

Two years,

Four months,

Seven days.

"I'm here," you say.

No response.

We're just two anonymous people at an impasse in a doorway.

Selected Poems

Flavia Rocha

From the series *To our Poets*

(to Orides Fontela)

I left some roses here, near the end.
But they didn't sound real,
they seemed human. They behaved like words,
with their cold curves and hard angles, arrows
of sound inside a box. You say FLOWER
with such cruelty. You make me understand
why every rose is an ex-rose.

(para Orides Fontela)

Coloquei rosas aqui, perto de algum final.
Mas não soavam reais,
pareciam humanas. Comportavam-se como palavra,
naquela frieza de curvas e ângulos contidos, flechas
de som dentro de uma caixa. Você diz FLOR
na crueldade crua. E me faz entender
porque toda rosa é ex-rosa.

From the series *To our Poets*

(to João Cabral de Melo Neto)

You clean the apple
from what's not knife: twenty slices
of the same apple split into twenty words.
But a bark suddenly breaks the crystal
and returns the whole dog to us, sanguine
and mystical, like a plump fruit dropping
into the swamp. And that river gets much thicker inside the man.

(para João Cabral de Melo Neto)

Você limpa a maçã
do que não é faca: vinte lâminas
da mesma maçã separam as vinte palavras.
Até que um latido quebra o cristal
e nos devolve o cachorro inteiro, sanguíneo
e místico, como uma enorme fruta que despenca
no mangue. E aquele rio fica muito mais espesso no homem.

From the series *Animalia*, in reference to the painting *Lei da Selva*, by Luiz Zerbini.

[untitled]

A plant in the center of the tropical
square, *macunaímica*
A plant in the conic silence of flowers
native, on a black ruler.
A pop plant flushing purple in trash
bags, yellow in the river.
A plant flattened against the wall
showing some fur.
A crushed plant, corked.
A plant. A pla. A.

A planta no centro do quadrado
tropical, macunaímica.
A planta no silêncio cônico das flores,
inata, na régua preta.
A planta pop pondo roxo no saco
de lixo, amarelo no rio.
A planta planificada contra a parede,
exibindo a pelugem.
A planta quebrada, engradada.
A planta. A pla. A.

all poems translated by author

Besieged

Sue Scavo

"Ah Sweet Soul," says Love, "You know more than you are saying."

Marguerite Porete
from *The Mirror of Simple Souls*

you are here   *to annihilate*   to shatter
to bring fire   must I   *be blaze*
lose myself   *lose what is not*   am I not
you are here   will there be   *I will bear*
anything left   *all that remains*

***

I feel   *begin*   your burning
with burning   can't stop   *surrender*
can't breathe   *ignite*   you are taking
let howl   the longing   *let tremble*
the anguish   *leave it*   all I have

***

I offer   what are you   *freedom*
what am I   *to bear*   it burns
the past   you burn   *the present*
I burn   *the future*

***

If no anger   *no anger*   if no anguish
no anguish   if no longing   *belonging*
if you as real   *no doubts*   you are
not me   *you of me*   if not peace
me of you   this burning   *to bear*

***

am I intact   *you are*   I believed
as blaze   in obliteration   *as light*
why am I   *alone*   still here
uncontainable   surely more   *as lover*
to sacrifice   *to receive*

Contributors

Rosa Alcalá is the author of three poetry collections, most recently *MyOTHER TONGUE*. Her poems are included in *American Poets in the 21st Century: Poetics of Social Engagement* (eds., Claudia Rankine and Michael Dowdy), among other anthologies. The recipient of an NEA Translation Fellowship and a finalist for a PEN Translation Award, she is the editor and co-translator of *Cecilia Vicuña: New & Selected Poems*. She teaches in the University of Texas at El Paso's Bilingual MFA Program.

Laylah Ali (Cover Artist) lives and works in Williamstown, MA. Her paintings, "Greenheads" have been included in the Venice Biennale (2003) and the Whitney Biennial (2004) and were the subject of a major touring exhibition in 2012-2013. Ali's works are included in the permanent collections of numerous public institutions, including the Albright-Knox Art Gallery, Buffalo, NY; the Museum of Contemporary Art Chicago; the Museum of Modern Art, New York; and the Walker Art Center, Minneapolis.

Nicole Callihan's books include *SuperLoop* (Sockmonkey Press 2014), and the chapbooks: *A Study in Spring* (2015), *The Deeply Flawed Human* (2016), *Downtown* (2017), and *Aging* (2018). Her poems have appeared or are forthcoming in *Tin House*, *Sixth Finch*, *Painted Bride Quarterly*, *The American Poetry Review*, and as a "Poem-a-Day" selection from the

Academy of American Poets. Her project *Translucence*, a dual-language, cross-culture collaboration with Palestinian poet Samar Abdel Jaber, was released by Indolent Books in 2018. Find her on the web at www.nicolecallihan.com.

Lucas de Lima is the author of *Wet Land* (Action Books) and the chapbook *Terraputa* (Birds of Lace). His writing has appeared or is forthcoming in *PEN Poetry*, *Poetry Foundation*, *boundary2*, and *Apogee*, and anthologies pertaining to Latinx, avant-garde, and eco-poetics. He is a doctoral candidate at the University of Pennsylvania and the recipient of a fellowship from the Social Sciences and Humanities Research Council of Canada.

Nathalie Handal's most recent books include the flash collection *The Republics*, lauded as "one of the most inventive books by one of today's most diverse writers" and winner of the Virginia Faulkner Award for Excellence in Writing and the Arab American Book Award; the bestselling bilingual collection *La estrella invisible / The Invisible Star*; the critically acclaimed *Poet in Andalucía*; and *Love and Strange Horses*, winner of the Gold Medal Independent Publisher Book Award, which The New York Times says is "a book that trembles with belonging (and longing)." Handal is a Lannan Foundation Fellow, Centro Andaluz de las Letras Fellow, Fondazione di Venezia Fellow, winner of the Alejo Zuloaga Order in Literature, and Honored Finalist for the Gift of Freedom Award, among other honors. She is a professor at Columbia University and writes the literary travel column "The City and the Writer" for *Words without Borders*.

Andrea Jeftanovic Avdaloff is a Chilean writer. Born in Santiago in 1970, she is considered one of the most prominent authors of her country. She is the author of the novels *Escenario de Guerra* (2000) and

Geografía de la lengua (2007), and of two volumes of short stories: *No aceptes caramelos de extraños* (2013) and *Destinos errantes* (2016). Of Jewish and Serbian ancestry, Jeftanovic grew up among three religions – Russian Orthodox, Catholic and Jewish. She studied sociology at the Catholic University in Santiago de Chile and in 2005 she finished a doctorate in Hispano-American literature at the University of California, Berkeley. Jeftanovic is not afraid of controversy, and sees art as "a space for moral experimentation." She has received several awards, including the Chilean Art Critics Circle Award and the National Book and Reading Council Award. Her work has been translated into several languages and it appears in foreign as well as national anthologies. She is a researcher at the University of Santiago, teaches literary workshops at the Gabriela Mistral Cultural Center among others, and writes about theater for *El Mercurio* newspaper.

Shay Lawz is a writer and performer raised in Jersey City, NJ. Her work has appeared or is forthcoming in *Big Big Wednesday*, *Winter Tangerine*, and elsewhere. She thinks often about the relationship between text and performance, sound and image, the body and everything else that we call home. She is a recent graduate of Brown University's MFA program and the 2018 Roxane Gay poetry fellow at Jack Jones Literary Arts. Currently, she is at work on an interdisciplinary project. You can find more at shaylalawz.com

Leila Christine Nadir is an Afghan-American artist, writer, and educator. She is the author of award-winning essays and artworks about public health, the Afghan diaspora, environmental theory, and her personal experiences of religion, ethnicity, trauma, and healing. Her primary project right now is her childhood memoir, titled *Bad Muslim*, which chronicles growing up within the colorful, turbulent marriage of her Afghan, Muslim father and Slovak-American, Catholic mother, who together raised seven children. Excerpts have appeared in *Aster(ix)*, *North American Review*, *Asian American Review*, and *McSweeney's Internet Quarterly*. She earned her PhD in literature from Columbia University, and is currently an Assistant Professor at University of Rochester, where she is also Founding Director of the Environmental Humanities Program. More info about her work can be found at http://leilanadir.xyz/.

Vi Khi Nao was born in Long Khánh, Vietnam. She is the author of *Sheep Machine* (Black Sun Lit, 2018), *Umbilical Hospital* (1913 Press, 2017), *A Brief Alphabet of Torture*, which won FC2's Ronald Sukenick Innovative Fiction Prize in 2016, the novel *Fish in Exile* (Coffee House Press, 2016), and the poetry collection *The Old Philosopher*, which won the Nightboat Books Prize for Poetry in 2014. She holds an MFA in fiction from Brown University, where she received the John Hawkes and Feldman Prizes in fiction and the Kim Ann Arstark Memorial Award in poetry.

Juan Carlos Reyes was born in Guayaquil, Ecuador. He's the product of a math degree, though only words hold his attention anymore. His first book, *A Summer's Lynching*, won the Quarterly West 2016 novella prize, and his chapbook, *Elements of a Bystander*, won the 2017 Arcadia Press Chapbook Prize. His stories, poems and essays have appeared in *Ascentos Review*, *KGB Lit*, and *Hawai'i Review*, among others. He is currently a Jack Straw Fellow and serves as an assistant professor of creative writing at Seattle University.

Flávia Rocha is the author of three poetry books published in Brazil: *A Casa Azul ao Meio-Dia* (Travessa dos Editores, 2005), *Quartos Habitáveis* (Confraria do Vento, 2011) and *Um País* (Confraria do Vento, 2015).

She has an M.F.A. in Writing/Poetry from Columbia University. For 13 years she was an editor then editor-in-chief for the multimedia literary magazine *Rattapallax*, based out of New York City. She is also a screenwriter, and a founder/Director of Communications of Academia Internacional de Cinema, a film school with branches in Sao Paulo and in Rio de Janeiro, Brazil. She currently lives in Portland, OR.

Malvina Sammarone is a visual artist who transits through drawing, photography, video and installations; where time, duration, unpredictability, chance,repetition, and process always permeate her works. She graduated in Architecture at Universidade Mackenzie and has an MA in Arts from New York University. Since the early 80s attends art courses and photography, artists workshops and study and orientation groups.

Sue Scavo is a poet, writer and teacher of the dream. She is also the Co-Founder/Editor of Deluge Journal, a literary and arts magazine dedicated to the creative work inspired by the dream or the dream-like realm. Her work has appeared in numerous journals such as Poet Lore and Blue Heron Review and anthologies such as *What Have You Lost* (ed by Naomi Shihab Nye). As a teacher of Embodied Dreamwork, Sue has taught for over 17 years all around the U.S. and Canada at centers such as Kripalu, Esalen, Breitenbush, and Hollyhock.

Olivia Rose Walton is a writer from South Africa currently living in London. She used to work as a journalist in Istanbul.

Acknowledgments

Flavia Rocha, "Selected Poems." Originals in Portuguese appeared in "Um País" (Confraria do Vento, 2015).

For Vi Khi Nao's The Proscenium: Preface, THE LAUNCH:
Typewriter image from:
http://site.xavier.edu/polt/typewriters/tw-parts.html
Uterus diagram from:
http://holyoak.co/uterus-diagram-unlabeled.html

Cover art is detail from "Sky" by Laylah Ali, gouache on paper, 2014.

www.ingramcontent.com/pod-product-compliance
Lightning Source LLC
Chambersburg PA
CBHW032041180726
48284CB00008B/2688

9781942547099